Someday I'll Be a Queen

TOOLBOX

PLAYING CHESS WITH A GROUP

Content

Insights for the coach of a group.

1. Why Learn Chess?

Chess is not just a game. When you observe children playing, you'll be amazed at how beneficial this game is for their overall development. I have had the privilege of witnessing and experiencing this firsthand. Chess not only stimulates thinking skills but also exercises various other aspects of functioning, such as social skills, spatial and mathematical understanding, concentration, shaping of self-image, and more.

Through chess, children learn to make plans and execute them, believe in themselves, persevere, or realize when their strategy is not working. Rational decisions need to be made. It is necessary to focus on what is important and adjust one's behavior or thoughts to achieve the desired goal. When the game takes unexpected turns, children learn to cope with mental flexibility and stress. In other words, children are given the opportunity to train their executive functions.

Reflecting on the added value of this chess book, Bert van der Spek, a former teacher at the Pedagogical Academy in the Netherlands, posed the following question to me: "In what way can we best educate children so that they can manifest themselves as optimally as possible in this complex world when they reach adulthood?" His answer is clear: "For primary education, parents have a crucial educational task (hopefully, they can take on this responsibility as well as possible). As the child grows older, they increasingly come into contact with informal educators, and once they start school, this phenomenon becomes stronger. The teacher then plays a vital role in contributing to the emotional, social, and cognitive development of the child. Later on, the school will provide support for a balanced co-education without losing sight of the primary responsibility of the parents. However, the school contributes to a pedagogical-didactic climate where skills are trained, such as numeracy, language, spatial and visual understanding, use of (working) memory, planning, forward thinking, mathematical thinking, creative problem-solving, and addressing challenges that the child - and later the adult - has never encountered before... Do you shy away from it or do you confront it?"

From birth, babies possess primary genetically inherited skills. These competencies are further influenced by significant environmental factors after birth and continue to develop. In my opinion, this chess method aligns well with the brain development - the thinking power - of individuals, especially in the case of preschoolers. *Bert van der Spek*

1.1. Who Am I And How Do I Fit Into the World?

Chess is an asset for the overall development of a child, but how do you notice this? How does a child attain self-knowledge and control over their own functioning? Children quickly realize through chess that they have to make choices. "Which chess piece should I move?" This choosing process can cause discomfort for some. "I don't know or I can't do it" are common statements. Through this game, they experience that making a choice can have consequences, both positive and negative. You can reassure and encourage them by saying that you will teach them to make good choices. However, it requires calm and careful thinking, as well as plenty of practice. It provides an opportunity to teach them how to deal with making mistakes. **Making mistakes is not a problem at all; you can learn from them and become stronger.** It goes without saying that impulsive children benefit from playing this game: think first, then act.

The game of chess is a great way to learn how to deal with these situations. I have often met children who gained control over their emotional outbursts or anger through chess. This is especially true when they look forward to participating in a school chess competition organized annually by the Belgian chess leagues of the 5 Flemish provinces. A temper tantrum is not appropriate there!

It is important to teach children that winning the game is not about being the smartest, but about thinking carefully and playing with concentration. **Gifted children who naturally learn quickly may sometimes confront themselves in this regard.** They might lose to a less "smart" or younger child because the other child thinks longer or reacts less impulsively.

The children learn from your communication style. How you talk or respond to others is important! During chess, it's better not to use words like "smart or dumb moves." They have a different meaning than "wise or thoughtful decisions." Also, do not allow children to react to each other in this way. The loser should not feel "dumb" because of mean comments but can assess for themselves whether enough attention was given to what happened on the chessboard (young children tend to look away from the game) or whether to apply a different strategy.

Social skills are extensively addressed in chess. How do you interact with your opponent? How do you present yourself? Are you afraid or do you have a lot of self-confidence? What do you convey? Can you manage to shake hands after the game, etc...? Indeed, within the chess world, every game starts with a handshake where the players wish each other "have fun" or "good luck." After the game, they shake hands again and congratulate each other on the effort made. Even if you have lost, being able to say, "Well played" or "Thank you for the game" means a lot!

Children who struggle with social interactions sometimes understand better how to approach something when you bring in the chess rules. In a conflict, they can respond as in chess: take a step back (walk away) from the conflict, put someone in between (protect your piece, get help), or counterattack (not literally, but symbolically by saying that you won't let others walk all over you).

Teacher and chess coach Tania Folie explains in a beautiful article how chess can make a child more resilient against bullying: *'Pesters-schaakmat'* (Bullies-checkmate). You can find this article at https://hetwittepaard.be/pesters-schaakmat/

Children who have difficulty fitting in with friends on the playground because they mainly engage in imaginative play or football are often happy to have a chess corner set up at school! The rules are clear there, and winning or losing depends entirely on oneself. **Through chess, you can see an increase in self-confidence in some children!**

Don't think that chess is only suitable for intellectually strong children or children who naturally excel in learning. Children with ASD (Autism Spectrum Disorder), dyslexia, dyscalculia, ADHD, behavioral disorders, or emotional problems can be quite good at chess! The longer they play chess, the more their self-confidence grows, and the better they learn to control their emotions.

Children who don't believe in themselves (anymore) find solace in the idea that even the Pawn – the smallest piece on the chessboard – can become a Queen!

1.2. Mathematical Thinking

When we look at the development goals for preschool age, we primarily focus on the subject area of "space". However, mathematical concepts are also addressed: the value of the chess pieces, for example, is expressed in numbers.

Preschoolers regularly count how many pieces they have captured, compare them with their opponent, and count again.

We practice concepts such as next to, in front of, behind, straight, diagonal, forward, backward, as far as possible, etc. These concepts are not fully ingrained at the age of 4 or 5, but they are introduced through play. The mathematical vocabulary is expanded by using terminology such as "broken line, diagonal"... Spatial awareness is developed through chess....

1.3. Brain Development

Studies show that during chess, metabolism increases, nerve cells become more active and start communicating with each other. Networks are activated during chess, according to clinical neuropsychologist Erik Scherder (website sport.nl).

"I'm mentioning only a few areas frequently used during chess. The frontal lobe for planning, flexible thinking, letting go of previous thoughts, and learning from mistakes. And the parietal lobe, which is essential for information processing."

The connections between these brain regions enable communication and the sharing of information necessary for a task. Chess helps children think better, analyze better, concentrate, and develop a strategy to reach a solution. The fact that these connections are more dynamic in the brains of chess experts than in those of novice chess players indicates that regular chess playing can improve brain communication.

"Chess is fantastic for everyone, especially for children and young people. By playing chess, you build up a cognitive reserve that you can tap into later when your brain declines, to protect yourself against age-related diseases", says Scherder.

2. Considerations

2.1. Why Learn in This Way?

You might think: why working with all those mini games and not just explain the rules of chess in an ordinary instruction? This approach can work, and I did it for a few years in a first-grade class. Spending ten minutes a day presenting something on an instruction board and doing some exercises is possible. You can capture their attention during that short instruction time. By the end of the school year, the 6-7-year-olds knew the basic rules.

However, if you want to try it with younger children, you need a narrative framework. When I tried to introduce the chess rules to preschoolers, I noticed that whole-class instruction or practice didn't work well. Preschoolers require a different approach.

They must feel it, experience it, live it, be stimulated by the drawing, the story, or a character so that it remains captivating. This book originated from that experience! This picture book is a mix of a story and chess rules so that preschoolers are introduced to the world of chess. The characters are lively and imaginative. Even the smallest chess piece - the Pawn - plays an important role in the story.

2.2. Why Start So Young?

Wouldn't it be better to wait until they are seven or eight years old? I have noticed that it is beneficial to introduce this in kindergarten. On the one hand, there is more time available in the weekly schedule of a kindergarten class, as the curriculum of a first-grade class is often packed. On the other hand, it is an opportunity to teach preschoolers something new that can be used as differentiation in elementary school for children who have completed their tasks or need an extra challenge. Imagine a child moving on to first grade already able to count to 10 or read. Why not engage this child with a chessboard or chess exercises?

Furthermore, there is a third good reason: mature preschoolers, gifted preschoolers, preschoolers with concentration problems, insecure children, etc. can be identified while introducing chess. My observations during chess lessons often confirm the perceptions that kindergarten teachers already have of their children. "This child has insight, thinks ahead, has good spatial perception... or "This child has difficulty concentrating, gets angry quickly, can't handle losing..."

3. 3. Getting Started: Introducing the Chess Pieces One By One Through Games

3.1. Preliminary

The more attention you can give to each child, the more you can adapt to their level. As a parent, grandparent, therapist, or chess coach, you can easily work with this book.

But I also address teachers or guides of young children because I want to share my classroom experience. In this way, I hope that educators see the value of this game and engage with chess.

I tried to come up with variations in my lessons because I work with very young children (+4) and want to keep preschoolers engaged. Some games that work well with preschoolers have been included in this book with permission from Cor van Wijgerden. The goal of each game is described alongside the chess piece being introduced.

If you want to know which learning objectives you can achieve through chess, you can find a lot of information about this on websites related to chess in schools.

Take the time to practice the games! **The intention is to repeat a game,** especially when the children enjoy it. So don't rush to the next game or a new chess piece too quickly.

If a game is perceived as difficult, take a break and play a lighter game in between, then return to the exercise later.

In kindergarten, I take two years to introduce all the basic rules by repeating a game every week and building from there. I usually work with a maximum of eight children, which allows all the kids to stay engaged in the game. Every child is unique, and so is every class group. Some children learn quickly, while others need more time. Try to understand what your children need. You could even divide your class into groups based on their skill levels. Choose the games that will likely be most successful for each chess piece or play them all for variation.

However, don't expect four-year-old preschoolers to have an overview of the chessboard. Children of that age don't have that perspective yet. They are mainly focused on the intriguing pieces and not so much on the flow of the game, attacking moves, or checkmate. This comes in a later stage.

Nevertheless, it is good to bring their attention to it. The different possibilities of a move can be visually represented to gain insight into the game. You can do this by placing objects on the squares where the chess piece is allowed to move. It could be a disc, block, bottle cap, or coin.

If you buy or create a life-sized chessboard (using painted outdoor tiles, spraying a weed control fabric with paint, or purchasing foam tiles), you can allow the child to physically experience what we mean by straight or diagonal lines. **This is called active learning.**

This way the children are invited to step into the role of the characters, which helps them recall and apply the chess rules from memory.

One of the most difficult chess pieces to introduce is the Horse*, it's the only chess piece that can jump into eight possible directions.

With young children, the Knight's move is often a challenging concept. I have searched for countless variations (and rhymes) to teach them that move. The choice for the rhyme that is now in the book was made with the children. It sounded the most beautiful to them and was best understood.

The support of the picture book combined with the rhyme will definitely add value!

The Knight being the correct chess term used

3.2. Special Moves Or Positions

These are not covered in this book. Once the preschooler knows and has practiced the basic rules, they will be ready to tackle more extensive exercises through other chess books for young children.

The chess book you have in your hands has been deliberately created for the very young ones. Its purpose is to stimulate their curiosity and teach them the moves of the chess pieces in a playful manner.

3.3. Point Value

Chess pieces are assigned a point value to demonstrate that some pieces are more powerful than others. This point value is not arbitrarily chosen but based on the experience of chess players over hundreds of years.

Young children are not initially concerned with this point value; for them, "capturing" is important. They may capture a Pawn but lose their Queen in the process... and they don't mind. Until they learn that it is better to protect the important pieces.

In my experience, some preschoolers become fixated on this point value because they think they need to collect the most "points". It can be a goal in itself as a game; who can collect 20 points the fastest? But it sometimes distracts them from the real goal: winning by checkmating the King! Therefore, you can choose not to discuss point values yet and only introduce it after presenting all the chess pieces.

Why do you talk about the point value?

- To emphasize the importance of strong and weaker pieces.

- To gain understanding of "trading" in chess; for example, you capture the Queen but in doing so, you lose a Bishop. In that case, you still made a gain.

    The Pawn is worth one point.

    The Knight is worth three points.

    The Bishop is worth three points.

    The Rook is worth five points.

    The Queen is worth nine or ten points.

    The King is infinitely valuable because if you trap it, you lose the game.

3.4. Rows and Files

At the bottom of the chessboard, you will find letters, and on the sides, you have numbers. This allows for easier naming of squares, such as "Place your chess piece on e1".

Horizontally, we refer to rows, and vertically, we call them files (or columns). A chessboard is set up correctly when the white square h1 is located in the bottom right corner, the white chess pieces are on rows 1 and 2, and the black pieces are on rows 7 and 8.

Introducing this information to preschoolers is difficult and not essential to playing the game. You can certainly share it if the child shows interest, but I included it here so that as a guide, you can position the chess pieces correctly. This is important for some of the games.

3.5. Guiding a Group Game

When playing individually with a child, it's not difficult to take turns moving a chess piece. However, in a group game, this can be more challenging.

You naturally want to give all children a chance to play and stay engaged by letting them take turns, so they don't have to wait too long. But... you also need to consider the alternation between playing as White and playing as Black!

As long as no player's piece is captured, you can maintain a good order. But once a piece is taken out of the game, it becomes a bit more complicated.

Let's consider an example: suppose you have six players designated in the order of white - black: white (Finn), black (Rick), white (Mike), black (Ahmed), white (Freya), black (Liv). If Ahmed is taken out of the game because his piece is captured, the order changes. Freya is temporarily skipped since you can't have two consecutive white moves, so Liv takes her turn. Then you can assign the turn to Freya, and the game continues: a black player (Rick), a white player (Finn)… It's not always easy for a facilitator to keep track of this, and mistakes can happen. The children usually don't mind, and it helps when you keep the overarching goal in mind: experiencing how the chess pieces move and thus remembering the rules. In these games, the focus isn't on building a full game or winning!

For an adult chess player, it's naturally challenging to prioritize the children's turn order over strategic moves. Sometimes, you might feel inclined to intervene by pointing out a different child's turn because of a situation on the board that you, as an individual player, would anticipate. You could briefly address it, then continue with the turn rotation.

Here's another example: Mike is playing the role of the White Queen and lines up with Liv, who has the Black Rook. In a regular game, the opponent would move the Black Rook to capture the Queen. However, in the group game, it's not Liv's turn; it's Ahmed's turn, and he cannot capture the Queen. As a result, the game evolves differently. That's what makes it interesting!

If the children are capable of discussing the situation and you ask who can make the best move, with preschoolers, you'll often get the answer "me." They want their turn and are not yet focused on the strategic development of the game.

3.6. Playing with the King

(see pages 32 to 37 of the picture book)

*Let's agree now that
we won't capture the Kings!
You can capture them,
but the game is not over yet!*

The starting position on the chessboard: revisit the pages about the steps of the King and discover together with the children where it starts on the chessboard: the White King is on the black square e1, and the Black King is on the white square e8.

The King can move one step in any direction, and then he needs to take a rest.

Examine each King to see which squares this chess piece can move to on the chessboard. You can mark those squares by placing a disk (or another object) on them.

When starting and finishing any chess game do not forget to shake hands with your opponent.

The following games are aimed at practicing:
Introducing spatial concepts: forward, sideways, backward, next to, diagonal...
Learning and applying the concept of "capturing" (first "waking up," then "grabbing," and finally using the correct term, "capturing").
Understanding that Kings cannot be placed next to each other and, therefore, cannot capture each other.
Learning to take turns by moving the King one step at a time.

Game 1 K

The Black King Among the Sleeping Chess Pieces

Objective: The goal of the game is for the King to "wake up" (capture) all the white chess pieces as quickly as possible.

Description: In this game, you will introduce the story of King Black who goes for a morning walk in his land and wakes up all the chess pieces. They rise and leave the chessboard. We are the real-life chess pieces. We need one King, while the other children are the sleeping chess pieces. The King can optionally wear a crown, a T-shirt with a logo, or a cape to be recognizable to the group.

Materials: Choose the black king. The other children are the sleeping chess pieces that can be awakened (beaten). Depending on the number of participants, you may choose to give the remaining players the task of directing (moving) the king as described here in this game.

Progression of the Game: All chess pieces are allowed to be placed on any random square on the board. Explain that they have fallen asleep (similar to the story of Sleeping Beauty) and thus cannot be moved. The Black King goes on a journey or is directed by one of the remaining players. The players collaborate in this way so that the Black King can awaken (capture) all the other chess pieces as quickly as possible. The chess piece that gets captured is taken off the playing field and follows along the sidelines to observe how the game unfolds.

Something more challenging?

If things are going well, add the White King to the game. The White King will disrupt the Black King's game. The 'sleeping' pieces now become 'white' chess pieces.

Explain that from now on, we will only talk about 'capturing' and not 'waking up' pieces. During this game, the White King will protect his pieces. Discuss how he can do this by standing next to a white chess piece. This way, the Black King cannot capture that piece because two Kings cannot stand next to each other.

In this group game, you can explicitly instruct the White King to sound the alarm when the Black King gets too close! (You can even use a fun prop like a flag, a trumpet, or a raised sword in the air if needed.)

Take turns playing, starting with white and then black.

Here are some tips for Game 1:

"This chess piece I must take, because that spot is mine to make."

1. Focus on teaching the child how to make and verbalize one step in all directions. Emphasize that the goal is to understand and communicate the movement of the King.

2. When a piece is not being captured, point it out to the children and assess whether they have understood the game correctly. This helps reinforce the concept that capturing is optional and not always necessary.

3. Teach the children that capturing means gently pushing the opponent's piece off its square and replacing it with their own piece. The accompanying rhyme can aid in remembering this concept.

4. Encourage the children to handle the chess pieces carefully and avoid knocking them over. If pieces are accidentally displaced, it becomes difficult to track their original positions. Place captured pieces neatly at the side of the chessboard.

5. Don't rush to the next game too quickly. Play this game frequently and allow the children to become comfortable with the movements of the King before moving on to new challenges.

Game 2 K

The King Chooses His Soldiers

Objective: The Kings try to gather as many soldiers for their army as possible. The game ends when all the soldiers are removed from the board.

Preparation: Take a look at the page in the book that explains the rules for the King. The two Kings should not be too close to each other (there must be at least one square in between). The objective is to collect as many pieces as possible while adhering to this rule.

Materials:

 or

You'll need a white and Black King, and the other children will be the soldiers. Place a bench or a few chairs on both sides of the chessboard for those who will be tagged. Perhaps you have a crown or a T-shirt with the King's symbol on it to make his role clearly visible to the players. The other children will be the soldiers and can be chosen.

In this game, the children might have to wait for their turn to come around again. That is also a goal in itself!

Progression of the game: The two Kings take their correct positions (in the middle of the 1st and 8th rows on the opposite color) and shake hands: "Have fun." All the other children play the soldiers (without a color) and choose a spot on the board. The Kings take turns to move one step; this can be in any direction. When a chess piece is tagged, that child sits on a chair in 'the camp of that King,' and their army grows. The game continues until there are no more 'soldiers' left. Which King has the largest army at the end of the game? Have them shake hands after the game: "Well played or thank you for the game."

Game 3 K

Treasure Hunt!

Objective: The Kings must maintain distance while trying to reach the treasure as quickly as possible. Their helpers occasionally build a wall when they get too close to each other.

Preparation: Explain that there is a treasure on the chessboard. It can be anything: a doll, a car, a dinosaur, a real treasure chest, a cup, etc. Which King will reach it first? Place the treasure on the 4th rank and switch colors in the next game: the white player becomes black and vice versa.

First, let's set up a small chessboard. Place a king on the board and surround it with markers to create a protective wall. Mark the eight squares around the king with objects. This wall is meant to prevent the other king from getting too close. If the other king breaches this wall, it is considered lost.

Materials:

You'll need the white and Black King and eight large colored squares to indicate the walls on the board. The other children (helpers) are the wall builders assigned to one of the Kings. If the Kings are positioned opposite each other (with one square between them), the walls will overlap. Make sure the materials are suitable for this purpose. A treasure (car, doll, treasure chest, etc.) is also important!

Progression of the game: Place the 'treasure' on the chessboard at e7 and explain that you're curious to see which King will conquer it. The White King starts at c1, and the Black King at g1. Instruct the other children to stand outside the chessboard, ready to build a wall on the chess squares around their King. The other King is not allowed in those areas! Allow the Kings to try to touch each other when they get close. This gives them a real sense of what is close and far.

This game generates a lot of excitement! You can have the wall builders move after each move if you want. Everyone is active, has something to do, so it's incredibly fun to play.

It's possible that neither King can capture the treasure because they approach it simultaneously while maintaining the required distance. In this case, the Kings will share the treasure! In a real game of chess, it's also possible for the game to end in a draw. This occurs in a stalemate or when the opponent has insufficient chess pieces left. We call this a draw.

Children may sometimes take detours, allowing one of them to reach the treasure faster than the other. Discuss afterwards what the shortest or fastest route was. This game can be played multiple times, but they will quickly figure out the fastest route unless you introduce obstacles that the Kings must navigate around.

Game 4 K

"King, Watch Out for Cars!"

Objective: The King must not put himself in danger. He must watch where he walks while trying to reach the other side as quickly as possible.

You'll notice that I'm not formulating the goal as "learning to give check" or "checkmating". Because putting a King in danger is actually called "putting in check." It can be difficult for these beginner chess players to do it intentionally. Unless we use cars! Then they understand it very well.

Children often accidentally discover that their King is in danger. They are focused on capturing pieces. However, it doesn't hurt to remind them that they need to protect their King and take action first. At that moment, the rule of "once you make a move, it's done" no longer applies. A King must not put himself in danger, so he must be moved to safety first.

Preparation: Tell the children that we are going to play with cars on the chessboard. It may seem a bit strange, but there used to be a chariot in the game of chess! Ask the children what "danger" means... maybe they can relate it to traffic situations; we also watch out for cars. We don't walk in the middle of the street or cross without looking carefully. Kings should do the same.

When the King moves, he must be careful not to step into a dangerous street. The reverse can also happen: if a car ends up in the King's street, the King must move quickly.

The cars move like Rooks, in straight lines. Demonstrate this clearly. They don't just move diagonally or zigzag across the board.

Materials: The large chessboard, both Kings, two toy cars, and a T-shirt or crown.

Group Division: Divide the children into two groups - the White King's group and the Black King's group. Make the King recognizable with a T-shirt or a crown. The children collaborate and can discuss the best strategy with each other.

Progression of the game: Place the toy cars somewhere along the sideline, for example, at a4 and h5. Explain that these cars can only move forward or backward along a 'straight street.' This street consists of alternating white and black squares. When a car wants to change direction, it stops at the intersection. In the next turn, it can turn and proceed. You can use two lines on the car's roof to show the horizontal and vertical paths departing from each car.

The Kings start at their initial positions and listen to the instructions from their teammates. The King must reach the other side as quickly as possible, but the teammates can influence the game's course to make it challenging for the opponent.

Someone from the white group starts and decides whether to move the White King or a car. (The car is neutral, not affiliated with white or black.) Then someone from the black group takes a turn. If a car is placed on a row or line (street) where a King is located, the King must be brought to safety first! There is no other choice; the King must be rescued first.

Note: When a car is placed next to a King, it can capture the King. This way, a car is disabled. Regularly verbalize what you see: "Oops, you're in danger, or he/she is putting you in danger!"

When playing the game again, switch colors. Initially, white might have an advantage, but if the children think carefully, black can still win.

In this game too, it may happen that the Kings remain stuck in place because a car keeps moving to "cut off" the opposing King horizontally from the part of the board that lies in front of him. Pause the game and discuss what can still happen. You can even attach two strips in a cross shape on the roof of the car to clearly show the children that a straight line is formed horizontally and vertically from the car. Children don't always think about attacking vertically.

Also, point out other dangers to them: when they flee from one car, they must also keep an eye on the other car.

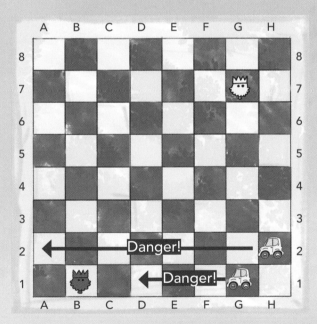

Finally: A checkmate position can accidentally occur. The King is at the edge, one car attacks him on that path, and the other car covers the adjacent path so the King cannot find safety there either (we call it a "staircase checkmate"). In that case, pause the game and show them the illustration from the book where the King lies on the "losing mat" (page 37). The King has nowhere to go; he is lost!

3.7. Playing with the Rook

(page 38 of the picture book)

point value
5

It slides across both colors,
First white, then black, again white and black.
It moves sideways or straight ahead, look...
it steps right over a pedestrian crossing!

The starting position on the chessboard: a Rook stands on each corner. The White Rooks are on a1 and h1, the black ones on a8 and h8. Take the picture book page 38 and reread the rhymes so that the children hear what a Rook can do. The Rook is straight and tall. That means it moves in straight lines and can slide as far as it wants: forward, backward, or sideways. If it encounters another chess piece on its path, it can capture it. It cannot jump over it. Naturally, it doesn't capture pieces of its own color!

Changing direction is not easy; the Rook must first stop and wait for its next turn. How do you teach this to young children?

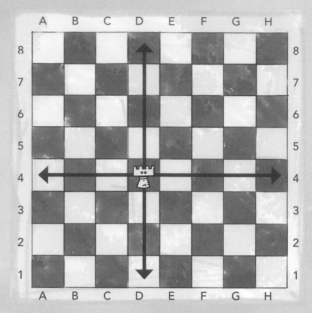

You can refer to the game with the cars, which drive in straight lines. It can't just take a turn! If we want to turn the car into another street, we often have to stop, look carefully, and then turn. After that, we can continue driving. That's how it is with a Rook too. If it wants to change direction, it must wait for its next turn!

You can also compare it to the Bee-bot or other programming materials if the children have already encountered them. The principle of going straight, stopping, and turning is then known or quickly understood.

In addition, it helps to visually mark the path the Rook will take. Let the child use strips, bars, or blocks to mark the path. The Rook's path is straight. If you make a turn in one move, you would have to crack the bar or bend the strip... the Rook would then be making a broken line. It's incredible how quickly some children adopt this wording during the game: "No, you're making a broken line, that's not allowed!"

When we let the children themselves play as a rook, they physically experience that they need to stay in one place and wait for their next turn to change direction. They begin by stepping sideways in a straight line to complete their move. Alternatively, they might start by moving sideways and then move forward or backward in the next turn. Some children might prefer to turn their bodies and then move forward again. I allow this but always articulate that it was good they waited for their next turn when changing direction.

When you make the path visually, the children will notice that a cross is usually formed originating from the Rook. For preschoolers who can already count, you can let them discover that the Rook can always go to fourteen squares, no matter where you place it.

You can practice this 'cross' by playing a game where you stand as a rook on the life-sized chessboard, and the children have to take a place on the rook's path. Then change your position, and the children figure out how the cross is formed again. Stand on a corner and see what happens.

Finally: Changing places in one turn is called "castling" (involving the Rook and the King). However, it is best to introduce this concept later as too much information might cause younger chess players to lose interest. We want to keep the children engaged, so it's advisable to cover "castling" in a different children's chess book or website. (Refer to the tips at the back of the book for recommendations).

Introducing spatial concepts: forward, backward, step sideways in the other direction.
Understanding that Rooks can move "as far as needed" without changing direction (not making a broken line).
Understanding that they cannot jump over obstacles or walls.
Understanding that you stay on the square where you capture an opponent's chess piece.
Learning to take turns by making one move at a time.
Collaboratively planning and visualizing a path. Which is the fastest route?
Executing the planned path using the Rook.
Reaching a predetermined square as the final goal.

Game 1 R

Programming the Rook

Objective: The White and Black Rooks compete against each other to see which Rook reaches the other side first.

Materials: the large chessboard, a White and a Black Rook (T-shirt). Something to create a barrier they can't cross: large blocks, stools, or other children sitting or lying down to form the obstacle.

Game progression: select two children to play the role of the Rooks. Dress them in white or black T-shirts to identify their roles as Rooks. This child will perform actions based on instructions from their "driver." Words like "rook move forward, Rook stop, Rook turn, or take two steps sideways" can help with this. Children familiar with programming will recognize this.

It gets even more fun when a "driver" is allowed to manually move the chess piece by placing their hands on the Rook's shoulders and guiding them. This approach is also simpler for children who may not be as verbal.

The game objective remains the same: ensure that the Rook reaches the other side from the starting position. It can move backward, sideways, or forward. If moving sideways is challenging, the Rook can stop and rotate the chess piece 90° to move forward in the next turn. Since the Rook only needs to reach the other side, there are eight possible "destination squares," making the game simpler.

Something more challenging?

My experience is that children often think about moving forward. Compare the steps on a small chessboard. Does the Rook rotate when it changes direction there? No, actually, we can just as well have the Rook move sideways. That's also changing direction.

- Practice the game in this way so they realize that Rooks can move sideways, forward, or backward! Explicitly instruct them to use these directions, for example: now the Rook must move backward as much as possible to reach the other side.

- Once they have a good grasp of the game, you can ask them to watch out for each other: if you're in the path of the other Rook, it can capture you!

- Then, make it even more challenging by using two Rooks of each color, which will make them encounter each other more frequently. Remove the obstacles if it becomes too complex.

- Or, if you add a King to the game, can they still accomplish the goal? Experiment with the chess pieces the children is familiar with. Discuss which chess pieces need to watch out for each other (pieces of the same color are part of the same "family" so they cannot be captured by each other). Repeat this information frequently during practice.

Game 2 R

Rook, Find the Best Path!

Objective: In this game, the goal is not simply to reach the other side with eight possible destination squares. Now, the Rook needs to land on a specific predetermined square! Explain that you will work together and discuss the best path. You will listen to each other and realize that there are multiple possibilities, expanding your thinking.

Materials: Two objects indicating the starting and ending positions (colored bean bags, for example). Folding rulers, wooden planks, or rope. Objects to build a wall. A Rook (color doesn't matter, we're working collaboratively at the beginning).

Game progression: Place two bean bags of the same color on the chessboard. These will indicate the start and end positions of the Rook, which is important for retrospective analysis. This way, the children can see where the Rook began.

Place several obstacles (see image) on the playing field. These can also be children who want to lie down or are assigned a spot by you.

Let the other children map out the path using rope, planks, or folding rulers. Then, the Rook starts sliding. It stops at each intersection. We count how many turns it takes for the Rook to reach the endpoint. Then, another child can map out a path from the starting position. Is this path faster? Are there more stopping points where they have to wait for the next turn?

If the game goes well, you can work without the visual path.

Something more challenging?

- If you wish, you can use numbers or multiple colored squares that need to be traversed in a specific order. Prepare this sequence next to the board (or draw it on cards beforehand) so that the children can see the pattern they need to follow.

- Let each child individually play the Rook. Now, they can't discuss anymore but make decisions on their own. Tell them they can also capture each other. They follow the path from their starting position to a colored bean bag, let's take 'red' as an example. When I play this for the first time, I give the child a red disc in their hands so they remember which bean bag is the destination, the red one. Then, I place the red bean bag somewhere on the chessboard (not in front of another Rook). As a guide, you need to look and think carefully here. I decide the position of the bean bag based on the challenge I want to give the child: easy or slightly more difficult. Now, the children have to be very careful not to get captured, as there might be five or six Rooks on the playing field! Game 3 T Collecting Discs Objective: collect as many discs or blocks as possible while making sure our Rook doesn't get captured. The game ends when all the discs are gone. (Even if there are still Rooks that can be captured.)

Game 3 R
Collecting Discs

Objective: Collect as many discs or blocks as possible while ensuring that our Rook is not captured. The game ends when all the discs are gone, even if a Rook can still be captured.

Materials and game progression: Same as the game above, but now the children play the Rook themselves. If you have multiple children in your group, you can let them control the Rook or play with the objects. Don't allow the children to push each other over. We don't knock over chess pieces!

Something more challenging?

When this game runs smoothly, you can introduce both Rooks to the game in their starting positions, which are the corners of the chessboard. Show the child that the Rooks are directly facing each other. This means that the White Rook could capture the Black Rook immediately. To prevent this, place a disc on lines a and h. Clearly explain to the children that the Rooks cannot capture each other because the disc is in between them. But once the discs are gone, they are facing each other! The next player's turn will allow them to capture the opponent's Rook.

Don't be surprised if the children, despite your warning, choose to immediately capture a disc; preschoolers often do that... They really want to conquer it! The realization that they lose a Rook by doing so comes later.

.

Game 4 R
King, Watch Out for the Rooks!

Objective: Now that the Rook's moves have been practiced, some additional thinking is introduced by bringing the King into the game! Here's what they need to do:

- The King must reach the endpoint (a treasure).
- The King must not be captured.
- The King must not be put in danger (by placing it in the path of the opponent's Rook).
- If the King is in danger, it must be brought to safety.

Information beforehand: With this game, you can introduce the concept of "check": if you place your Rook on the line (or street) where your opponent's King is, you are attacking that King. We call it "check". What can the King do then? Move away from that line, hide behind a wall if it's nearby, or place another Rook in between. Or if the King happens to be next to the attacking Rook, it can capture it! Demonstrate this on a small chessboard. The goal is not for the children to master the concept of "check" after this game. Give them more time for that! But they can become familiar with these moves in a playful way.

Materials: A White Rook and King, a Black Rook and King, and a treasure. If you have extra players, they can form obstacles by sitting or lying down on the chessboard. If you only have four players, you can use objects to create obstacles if you want to make the game a bit more challenging.

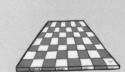

Game progression: Start by demonstrating on a small chessboard what you will be playing and what to pay attention to. This is an important phase! Once you are sure that the children understand, you can play on the large chessboard.

Place a White Rook on a1 and the White King on its starting position e1. The Black Rook starts at h8 and its Black King at e8. Place an object or 'treasure' on f6 where the White King needs to end up, and on d3 for the Black King.

Players can decide whether to move their Rook or their King. The player whose King reaches the treasure first wins, even if they have lost a Rook. Remind the children that losing the Rook makes the game more challenging for the King. If the King is in 'check,' they must focus on rescuing it in the next turn.

Indicate which child's turn it is, or let them decide through discussion by asking which chess piece should be moved. Refer to the information on guiding group play on page 6 of section 3.5.

You can consider replaying the game and placing obstacles on certain squares to make it even more exciting. Switch colors after each game: the white player becomes black and vice versa.

Slightly more challenging: Simultaneous chess with the group

The children will gradually be ready for simultaneous chess. This means you play against all the children at once. Arrange the children in a U-shape at different tables, each with a small

chessboard, white and Black Rooks, and Kings. Play game 3 of the Rook like an individual coach would. You act as the white player and make the initial moves for each board. Meanwhile, the children think about their countermove. They can only make their move when you return to their table.

This is a fun way to gain insight into the children's thinking, their understanding, and their individual responses while playing. With some children, I make challenging moves, while with others, I might overlook something to give them a sense of winning. "Mom, today I beat the teacher!" Especially for insecure children, this can be enjoyable and boost their self-confidence.

3.8. Playing With the Bishop

point value
3

(page 40 of the picture book)

Refer to the story again so that the children hear that the Bishop always stays on the same color. He finds his shoes very important. If he is wearing white shoes, he only stays on white. That's why a Bishop with black shoes has also been introduced because you always need a Bishop on both colors. Show both White Bishops and place them on different colors. Then show the two Black Bishops. This way, the children see that there are four Bishops in the game. Study the funny hat, which looks like Saint-Nicolas' miter, patron saint of children. We see a diagonal stripe on the hat, which reminds us that the Bishop always moves diagonally.

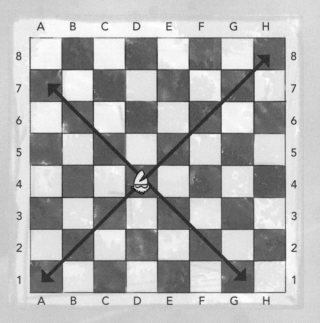

It is important to spend enough time on the understanding of "diagonal".

The squares on the chessboard touch each other at the corners and form a diagonal line: we follow the same color, so that means we walk to the corner of a square and step onto the next square. You can examine the Bishop's shoes in detail. They are pointy and refer to a corner of a chess square.

If you're using the large playing field, take the children for a walk and guide them over the diagonal squares. After a while, you can let the children walk diagonally on their own. Be careful: don't let them hop from one foot to the other, landing on black squares each time, for example, from b2 to c3 to b4 to c5... This way, they won't realize they are moving diagonally. Then they don't realize they're moving diagonally. Hopping in a zigzag manner is not allowed; the body needs to rotate and change direction like a robot.

The following games focus on practicing:
Introducing spatial concepts: diagonally forward, diagonally backward.
Understanding that Bishops can move "as far as necessary".
Knowing that Bishops stay on their own color throughout the game.
Understanding that you stay on the square where you capture a chess piece.
Learning to take turns by making one move.

You will notice that there are fewer games written out in this section. **Some games from the Rook section can be repeated with the Bishop.** I'm thinking of "Programming the Bishop", "Finding the Best Path", or "Collecting Discs". You will see that the children quickly grasp the task. Only the diagonal movement is new.

Tip: When setting up the chessboard, you need to think carefully about which color the Bishop should start and end on since the Bishop always stays on its own color! So, you cannot give a black squared Bishop the task of ending on a white square or picking up the disc on a white square.

In the game "Collecting Discs," you need to place an equal number of discs on black and white squares to ensure fair chances. Unless you have the White and Black Bishops moving on the same color. Then it's a race to see who reaches the treasure first.

Game 1 B

Bishop, Beware of the King!

Objective: The children practice sliding the Bishop over the correct color and following the diagonal lines. When the Bishop gets too close to the King, the King can capture it. In the first game, you play as the King.

Materials: A White Bishop on f1 (white), the Black King on d4 (black).

Game progression: Place a White King on e4 and the two Black Bishops on their starting positions. Let the Bishops start moving, but warn them not to get too close to the King, as he can capture them when they pass through a square adjacent to the King! Allow the children to move freely (without zigzag hopping), so you don't need to use names or take turns. It's a kind of "tag" game. Sometimes, the preschoolers find it very challenging to pass just next to the King. If he's quick enough, he can tag them. Then the Bishop is "captured." But maybe the Bishop is super fast! Still, you can intervene: shout 'freeze,' and the Bishop has to stop. Now, the King can take a step, putting him on a different colored square. Or shout "freeze" when a Bishop is right next to the King!?

At the end of the game, explicitly explain that today's activity was a tag game aimed at practicing diagonal lines. In regular chess, a Bishop must stop after each move and can only change direction on its next turn.

Game 2 B

The Bishop Takes on Two Rooks

Information beforehand: You will notice that the children get better and better at playing with the chess pieces, especially if you don't put too many "characters" on the board at once. In a chess match, a timer is usually used. It's not a bad idea to incorporate it as a game element. Not to stress the children, but to explain that it's good to agree on how long the game will last. Some chess players can spend hours on the same game if they don't use a clock. The longest game ever lasted 24 hours and 30 minutes, a day and a night!

Objective: The goal is simple: the Bishop must be captured before time runs out; otherwise, the Bishop wins.

Materials: Two children play as Black Rooks, and one child is the White Bishop. A timer or hourglass can be used, and other children can keep track of time. You can also involve them as 'controllers' of the chess pieces.

Game progression: First, demonstrate the game on a small chessboard. Discuss the strategic aspects of the game. Can our Rooks attack the Bishop every time? Where can you place your Rook to threaten the Bishop? (Compare with the King moving into the dangerous territory of the Rook).

Once the children understand the game, you can play it on the life-sized chessboard. Place the Rooks in their starting positions (the corners of the chessboard). Ask the child playing the Bishop which squares they want to move to, either white or black.

Emphasize the choice of the black or White Bishop and review the path again. The Bishop moves diagonally!

Afterward, take turns: Rook one makes a move, then the White Bishop makes a countermove. Rook two then takes a turn, followed by the Bishop, and so on.

Some children might not initially realize that they can attack the Bishop with their Rooks. Help them with that. By taking on the role of a Rook yourself, they will eventually see that they are indeed in the Bishop's path, attacking it!

The game usually ends when an inattentive Bishop ends up on a line with one of the Rooks. That's okay and quite typical for young children. Learning to cope with losing helps them overcome that frustration. When you switch roles afterward, the loss is often quickly forgotten.

If you're using a timer and the Bishop is not captured before the time runs out, then the Bishop wins!

Game 3 B

Running in Circles, Get Back to Your Starting Position as Fast as Possible

Objective: Make the chess pieces run around a wall and return to their starting position as quickly as possible. They should follow the correct path: the Bishop on diagonal lines and the Rook on straight lines. Show in advance the direction in which they should start (clockwise).

Materials: Chessboard, a White Bishop and Rook, and a Black Bishop and Rook. In the center of the chessboard, place a wall made of blocks or Pawns.

Game progression: The White Bishop is on a1, the White Rook is on b1, the Black Bishop starts on h8, and the Black Rook is on g8. White begins and makes a move, of course. The objective of the game is to 'run' along the wall (in a clockwise direction) and return to the starting position as quickly as possible. Who can do it the fastest? Capturing is not allowed. Then switch colors.

3.9. Playing with the Queen

point value

9

(page 42 of the picture book)

Straight lines and diagonal stripes,
or when she stands in the middle of the board.
She can reach up to twenty-seven squares.
No other chess piece can match that!

Take the picture book, page 43, and read the story again. Look at this illustration and tell how much the Queen loves to start on her own color. She has put on her most beautiful dress for that. This way, we can remember where she starts on the chessboard: next to the King on her own color. Since the Rook and Bishop are already known, it is very easy to transition to the dame (queen). She can move to the squares used by both the Rook and Bishop. Demonstrate this first on a small board. Place a Rook on d5 and let the child use colored discs to indicate the squares it can move to. Then replace the Rook with a Bishop and mark this path with different discs. Finally, replace the Bishop with a Queen and tell them that she can do both of these things together! The Queen is a powerful chess piece, let the child count the squares it can move to! On the large chessboard, you can also play a similar game. Stand somewhere on a square as a proud and powerful lady, and perhaps 'wearing a crown, being a Queen', and ask the

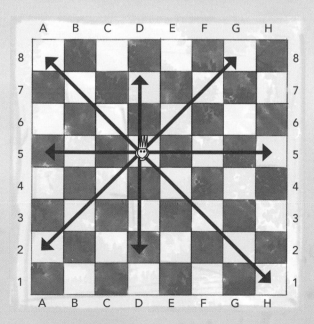

children to move to a square on one of the paths starting from the lady. Then, move to another square.

These games help practice:
Further practicing spatial concepts.
Looking at the path being taken: diagonal, sideways, straight, or backward.
Changing direction effectively: stopping first, then continuing on the next turn.
Being aware of dangers.
Learning to cope with frustration (the more chess pieces on the board, the more challenging the game becomes, and the more likely you are to miss something).

Game 1 Q

Celebration with the Queen

Objective: Explain that the Queen is hosting a celebration in her castle and personally picking up her friends to join in. She visits them one by one and takes them in her carriage. The children can fantasize about the type of celebration: a pancake party, a coffee gathering, a fries feast... They find it super exciting! But... will they arrive on time for the celebration?

Materials: A Queen and the guests (all the other children who sit on different squares of the chessboard), a timer or an hourglass.

Game progression: The Queen starts walking and passes by the guests. When she touches them, they stand up and follow her to the castle. They can even form a 'train', which they find amusing. Make sure the Queen always stands in the square of the chess piece she touches.

Also, ensure that the Queen follows the correct lines: either she chooses diagonal movement like the Bishop or the straight lines of the Rook. Ask the Queen to loudly announce to her guests which path she is taking: "I'm going diagonally, come with me."

Play this game first without a timer. When the children understand it well, you can gradually shorten the time they have. This game brings a lot of excitement. They enjoy it, and the rear guard usually follows the planned path quite well.

Something more challenging?

Add obstacles on the path or pieces from the opponent's side. They can capture the Queen! For instance, choose a Black Bishop and Black Rook. They don't move during the game but carefully guard 'their paths'. If the Queen passes over their squares, they can shout 'halt' and capture the Queen. However, the Queen can of course approach these pieces strategically and eliminate them. For instance, by approaching the Rook diagonally, it becomes powerless.

Game 2 Q

The Festive Table Is Set!

The party is starting for real. All the guests are gathered around the table, choosing the tastiest treats.

Objective: Who can capture the discs without getting captured themselves? Jumping over the discs is not allowed.

Materials: A White Queen and Rook, a Black Queen and Rook. Eight delicious treats (discs). The other children can be involved in controlling the chess pieces. If, for example, you have six children, one player controls the white pieces, and another controls the black ones. If you have more children, you can assign each chess piece a controller.

Game progression: Call out the players' names one by one, alternating between white and black. However, if the children are capable of coordinating, you can let them decide who makes a move.

After all the treats have been captured, calculate who has managed to capture the most delicious treats. Add up the point value of the remaining chess pieces for this purpose.

For example, if white has four treats and the Queen remaining, that player has 13 points. Switch colors and play the game again. Then tally up the final scores.

Something more challenging?

- Add a second Rook for both colors.
- Transition again to simultaneous chess. This way, the children gradually get used to playing on a small board. If this game is too challenging, opt for one of the previous games.

Game 3 Q

The Starting Position.

Objective: Practice the positioning of the chess pieces using all the pieces we have learned.

Materials: All the chess pieces we've learned so far for both colors: Rooks, Bishops, Queens, and Kings. Use a rope to indicate the half of the chessboard.

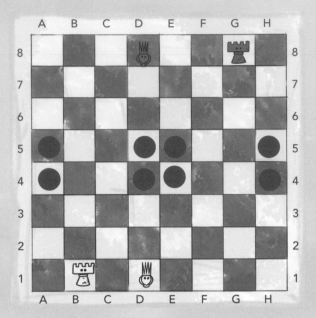

Information beforehand: If you don't have enough players for the large chessboard, create two teams (the white team against the black team). Have them sit on both sides of a smaller chessboard, for example, one with squares of 10 cm by 10 cm and chess pieces that are 20 cm tall (available in stores). If you don't have this, you can let the children

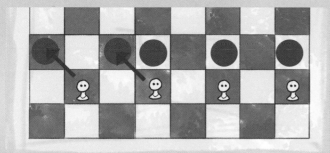

of a Pawn or diagonally in front of it.

"Ready, eyes open! Guess who can capture the discs?"

Let the children answer before executing a move. Their collaboration as a group is key. Introduce the concept of "touché," which means "touch is move." When playing a chess piece, the rule is "once touched, move made."

For example, if there's a disc on c3, both the Pawns on b2 and d2 can capture it. But if b2 goes first and captures on c3, then d2 can no longer capture that disc. Here, the group only captures one Pawn when there was a chance to capture two. If this is too complex, omit the "touché" rule for now.

Something more challenging?

Give the children extra discs and place them on other ranks. Now, the Pawn has to plan its path to the other side, considering which discs can be captured along the way. This action can change when a teammate captures the same disc. Exciting!

Game 3 P

Who Reaches the Other Side First?

Objective: The first to promote wins! You also win if your opponent can no longer move. Pay attention to capturing, which can only be done diagonally!

Materials: The large chessboard, divide the group into white and black players. Give them distinct shirts or something to indicate their colors.

Game Progression: Position the players on the board so that Pawns can be captured. Call each child's name in turn, starting with a white player and then a black one.

Observe what unfolds. The Pawns get close to each other!

In the next turn, they must collaborate as a group: who could make the best move now? One white player moves forward, then one black player. It becomes fascinating to hear the children discuss strategies with each other!

Something more challenging?

Have the children play against each other on a small chessboard or play simultaneous chess. Each child has their chessboard, and you move from board to board, making a move for white. Children can only move when you are in front of their board.

Steps Game 2P

Step 1: Set up the Pawns.

Step 2: Count how many pieces can be captured.

Step 3: Capture the pieces.

3.11. The Difficult Horse

point value
3

I twist my snout and then watch out:
I jump two steps forward and one aside
That's happens when a Knight is untied.

Refer to page 48 of the picture book.

There are many variations used in teaching the Horse's leap: two squares forward and one sideways or vice versa. Or one square in a straight line followed by one square diagonally. How difficult this is for young children! The concept of "diagonal" is completely beyond them. Trying to explain using the letter "L" is one possibility, but * for preschoolers who are not yet working with letters, this is also not an entry point. In the Batsford publication of Chess for Kids by Sabrina Chevannes, the word "ka-ta-klop" is proposed as rhythmic support. It's a fun idea, maybe it will work for your children.

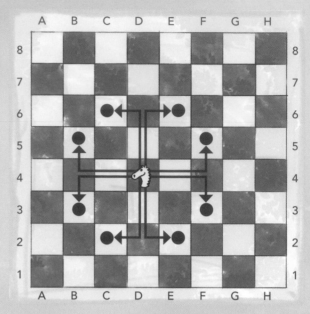

I have tried various games but eventually came to the conclusion that it's better to keep it simple; one strategy, for example, through a rhyme.

It's important to explain that the Horse always jumps to a different color on the chessboard and can turn its head in four directions. Show this on a small chessboard. I deliberately choose to position the head of the Horse in the direction it wants to go. This way, they concentrate on that path; they may turn the head again and again... Young children never think about making the Horse jump backwards at first. That comes later naturally.

To practice the movements of the Horse, you can play a few simple games with the children, pretending to be a Horse. "Because a Horse's eyes are on the sides, it can't always see well ahead. Shall we try to experience how that feels?"

- Walk around with your nose up, maybe play a tagging game. Can we see each other well walking with our noses in the air? No! A Horse has the same problem. That's why it recites the verse in chess, so it always ends up in the right place. It can jump as if blind! Let's try that too? Recite the verse with your eyes closed and meanwhile take the steps: "I turn my snout and take two steps forward, now one to the side, that one's definitely required..." Open your eyes and look. You're performing a dance step!

- Do you have a hobbyHorse? Then you can practice the concept of "to the side" with it if it's not understood. The rider takes one step "to the side" when dismounting. The children see that the eyes on the hobbyHorse are on the sides, those are the sides, emphasize that word.

The following games focus on:
Concepts: forward, sideways, addition.
The 4 "directions" in which the Knight can leap.
Role-playing and social interaction (taking directions and giving directions).
Memorizing the verse.
Following a path in the correct order or color.

Game 1 N

The Farmer Guards His Field

Objective: Visualize the position on the board by marking the landing squares for each leap of the Knight. Tell a story about a family that is worried about the Knight. It stands all alone in the meadow, and they are afraid it might escape! To prevent this, they decide to stand on all the spots where the Knight could land. Unfortunately, as evening approaches, they have to go to sleep and secretly hope that the Horse will sleep too. But that's not the case...

Materials: Large chessboard, a Horse (one child), other children (representing family members), or objects that children can place on the destination squares of the Horse.

Gameplay: Tell the story as described above. One child plays the role of the Horse and stands in the middle of the chessboard. Gather the other children together and say, "Quick, our Horse must not escape, stand on a destination square." Help the children find their designated squares. Recite the verse while doing this. Continue with the imaginative play. It's now bedtime: "Come, let's go to sleep and we'll be back tomorrow." Count how many destination squares the Horse has. There are eight possibilities in the center of the chessboard. The children leave the chessboard. Now, the Horse must leap to a suitable square without any visual help.

Panic upon waking up! The family discovers that the Horse is no longer in its original spot. It's still in the meadow but at a different place. Reassess the situation. The participants need to return to an arrival square. If the Horse is on the side, fewer children are needed to occupy squares. This way, they experience firsthand that fewer players are necessary.

Also, try putting the Horse in a corner. How many children can sit in a spot then? Much fewer! Play along by saying, "If your Horse is on the side, something is at stake." The Horse is indeed the strongest in the center of the chessboard.

And thus, the story repeats itself over and over again. After a few turns, let someone else play the Horse. Children find this game very enjoyable; they become fully immersed in it.

Game 2 N

Hey, Where Can I Leap To?!

Objective: Practice the Knight's leap and mark all the squares the Knight has visited. The Knight must not land on the same square twice.

Materials: Large chessboard, a Horse (one child), other children with objects like bean bags, blocks, etc.

a lot

Gameplay: The game proceeds as described above. The Horse takes its starting position on the chessboard. The other children stand beside the board, each holding an object. When the Horse starts its move, one of the children places their object on the square the Horse moved to. The objective is to see how far the Horse can go without getting blocked.

Game 3 N

The Horse is Hungry

This is a variation of the previous game. It is played in reverse: the game board is filled with discs. These represent the Horse's food (e.g., carrots). Now the Knight will leap and try to eat all the carrots as quickly as possible.

Something more challenging?

- Let two Knights participate: one white and one black. Be careful, they can capture each other!
- Create cards with numbers or number representations (according to the level of your children). Scatter them across the board. The Knight must follow the correct path to collect the cards one by one. Make sure the child recites the verse and, therefore, takes the correct path. This is not an easy task. Sometimes, a detour must be taken to reach the correct square! In a group game, you can send a rider along to make sure everything is going smoothly. The rider then guides the Horse's moves.
- There are fun apps available for practicing the Knight's leap. Consult your search engine for more information.

4. All Pieces Are in Place

How do you proceed once all the pieces have been covered? There are several possibilities:

- You can continue practicing with mini games (i.e. not all pieces on the board at once). In the next section, you will find some examples from the Steps Method by Rob Brunia and Cor van Wijgerden.

- Play a first full game, but assist the children in making choices. Try to verbalize a lot! Discuss the pros and cons of a move. Warn them if they overlook something important or provoke them by making a "wrong" move yourself... You can involve an older sibling to play together against you. Or is it the other way around, where you need to collaborate with your youngest children to defeat the eldest?

- Assist the children in making choices. Vocalize your thoughts! Name the pros and cons of a move. Warn them if they overlook something crucial, or provoke them by suggesting a "wrong" move yourself.

- Continue to explore simultaneous chess.

4.1. More Mini Games

Queen versus Knight

The White Queen needs to capture the black Knight. They start in their initial positions. It's not an easy task! However, as they practice the game, they can succeed. For example, when the Knight is in a corner.

Bishop versus Pawns

Place three white Pawns on a2, b2, and c2. Across the board, there is a Black Bishop on c8. White can start. The Pawn side wins if a Pawn promotes or if the Bishop is captured. The Bishop wins if all the Pawns are captured or if the last Pawn is blocked.

Promotion game

Set up the eight white Pawns in their starting positions. Across the board, there is a black Knight in its familiar spot, b8. When a Pawn reaches the opposite side, it promotes. This earns the white player a point. The Knight must capture as many Pawns as possible and prevent itself from being captured. After the first round, the players switch roles. Once this game is completed, the player with the most points is determined.

4.2. Encouraging Chess in School:

Chess is a game for all ages, and you can bring it to life throughout your entire school. Everyone, regardless of age, can appreciate each other's skills, as age doesn't always determine the winner.

- Create a Chess Corner: Designate an area on the school playground as a chess corner. This provides a space for children who aren't interested in activities like football or imaginative play to engage in chess and play together.

- Free Choice Time: During breaks or free choice periods at school, allow children to choose to play chess.

- Cross-Class Collaboration: Collaborative learning across classes is valuable. When starting with younger children on a smaller chessboard, involve older children to assist. This way, mistakes can be corrected immediately and correct moves reinforced.

- Participate in School Chess Tournaments: Enroll in school chess tournaments. Participation can ignite enthusiasm throughout the school.

- Support Interested Teachers: Provide support to teachers who want to introduce chess. Offer appropriate materials, including good chess books.

- Practice Books: The practice books from the Stappenmethode by Rob Brunia and Cor van Wijgerden are excellent for providing children with an extra challenge. These books are full of problem-solving exercises, and children must choose the correct solutions. They're ideal for differentiating instruction for advanced learners. These books are commonly used in chess clubs and can be very useful in a school setting. They also include assessments to help determine a child's chess skill level.

Promoting chess in school can not only enhance strategic thinking and problem-solving skills but also foster a sense of community and healthy competition. It's a versatile and educational activity that can benefit students of all ages.

4.3. Websites and Instructional Videos

By consulting your search engine, you can find numerous sources of information about chess. Be cautious with chess programs that require practicing against a computer, as they can be challenging, especially for children. It's important to find a suitable platform where children don't get lost or lose interest. Therefore, I recommend https://lichess.org.

While creating this book, I quickly realized that referring to some websites carries a risk. Links may work one day but not another. That's why I will share and update information on my own website to accommodate new developments or questions that arise. Visit www.kleuterschaken.be for this purpose.

On this site, you can watch instructional videos of the group games described in this book. The individual coach can also find photos of how to set up the various games. Some people prefer to see how it's done before trying it themselves. A picture is worth a thousand words. See how children enjoy the game, how the game progresses, and how to approach it.

Enjoy teaching and exploring the picture book together!

Tip: You can find a "losing mate" puzzle and a little dragon on many pages. Have you spotted them yet?

This book is related to the picture book "Someday I'll Be a Queen".

Would you like to order this book?
This book is available at most professional bookstores.

First edition ©2024 Thinkers Publishing

All sales or enquiries should be directed to Thinkers Publishing, 9850 Landegem, Belgium.
E-mail: info@thinkerspublishing.com
Website: www.thinkerspublishing.com

Copyright © 2024 Thinkers Publishing, Belgium
Author: Christel Minne
Managing Editor: Daniël Vanheirzeele
Translation: Daniel Fernandez & Daniël Vanheirzeele
Author's portrait: Jan Franco
Cover Design & Illustrations: Diriq
Graphic Design: Driedee Plus
Production: BestinGraphics
This book is printed on environmentally friendly paper.

When starting and finishing any chess game do not forget to shake hands with your opponent.

Someday I'll Be a Queen

TOOLBOX

PLAYING CHESS WITH ONE CHILD

Content

Insights for the individual coach (parent, grandparent, teacher, child).

1. Why Learn Chess?

Chess is not just a game. When you observe children playing, you'll be amazed at how beneficial this game is for their overall development. I have had the privilege of witnessing and experiencing this firsthand. Chess not only stimulates thinking skills but also exercises various other aspects of functioning, such as social skills, spatial and mathematical understanding, concentration, shaping of self-image, and more.

Through chess, children learn to make plans and execute them, believe in themselves, persevere, or realize when their strategy is not working. Rational decisions need to be made. It is necessary to focus on what is important and adjust one's behavior or thoughts to achieve the desired goal. When the game takes unexpected turns, children learn to cope with mental flexibility and stress. In other words, children are given the opportunity to train their executive functions.

Reflecting on the added value of this chess book, Bert van der Spek, a former teacher at the Pedagogical Academy in the Netherlands, posed the following question to me: "In what way can we best educate children so that they can manifest themselves as optimally as possible in this complex world when they reach adulthood?" His answer is clear: "For primary education, parents have a crucial educational task (hopefully, they can take on this responsibility as well as possible). As the child grows older, they increasingly come into contact with informal educators, and once they start school, this phenomenon becomes stronger. The teacher then plays a vital role in contributing to the emotional, social, and cognitive development of the child. Later on, the school will provide support for a balanced co-education without losing sight of the primary responsibility of the parents. However, the school contributes to a pedagogical-didactic climate where skills are trained, such as numeracy, language, spatial and visual understanding, use of (working) memory, planning, forward thinking, mathematical thinking, creative problem-solving, and addressing challenges that the child - and later the adult - has never encountered before... Do you shy away from it or do you confront it?"

From birth, babies possess primary genetically inherited skills. These competencies are further influenced by significant environmental factors after birth and continue to develop. In my opinion, this chess method aligns well with the brain development - the thinking power - of individuals, especially in the case of preschoolers. *Bert van der Spek*

1.1. Who Am I And How Do I Fit Into the World?

Chess is an asset for the overall development of a child, but how do you notice this? How does a child attain self-knowledge and control over their own functioning? Children quickly realize through chess that they have to make choices. "Which chess piece should I move?" This choosing process can cause discomfort for some. "I don't know or I can't do it" are common statements. Through this game, they experience that making a choice can have consequences, both positive and negative. You can reassure and encourage them by saying that you will teach them to make good choices. However, it requires calm and careful thinking, as well as plenty of practice. It provides an opportunity to teach them how to deal with making mistakes. **Making mistakes is not a problem at all; you can learn from them and become stronger.** It goes without saying that impulsive children benefit from playing this game: think first, then act.

The game of chess is a great way to learn how to deal with these situations. I have often met children who gained control over their emotional outbursts or anger through chess. This is especially true when they look forward to participating in a school chess competition organized annually by the Belgian chess leagues of the 5 Flemish provinces. A temper tantrum is not appropriate there!

It is important to teach children that winning the game is not about being the smartest, but about thinking carefully and playing with concentration. **Gifted children who naturally learn quickly may sometimes confront themselves in this regard.** They might lose to a less "smart" or younger child because the other child thinks longer or reacts less impulsively.

The child learns from your communication style. How you talk or respond to others is important! During chess, it's better not to use words like "smart or dumb moves." They have a different meaning than "wise or thoughtful decisions." Also, do not allow children to react to each other in this way. The loser should not feel "dumb" because of mean comments but can assess for themselves whether enough attention was given to what happened on the chessboard (young children tend to look away from the game) or whether to apply a different strategy.

Social skills are extensively addressed in chess. How do you interact with your opponent? How do you present yourself? Are you afraid or do you have a lot of self-confidence? What do you convey? Can you manage to shake hands after the game, etc...? Indeed, within the chess world, every game starts with a handshake where the players wish each other "have fun" or "good luck." After the game, they shake hands again and congratulate each other on the effort made. Even if you have lost, being able to say, "Well played" or "Thank you for the game" means a lot!

Children who struggle with social interactions sometimes understand better how to approach something when you bring in the chess rules. In a conflict, they can respond as in chess: take a step back (walk away) from the conflict, put someone in between (protect your piece, get help), or counterattack (not literally, but symbolically by saying that you won't let others walk all over you).

Teacher and chess coach Tania Folie explains in a beautiful article how chess can make a child more resilient against bullying: *'Pesters-schaakmat'* (Bullies-checkmate). You can find this article at https://hetwittepaard.be/pesters-schaakmat/

Children who have difficulty fitting in with friends on the playground because they mainly engage in imaginative play or football are often happy to have a chess corner set up at school! The rules are clear there, and winning or losing depends entirely on oneself. **Through chess, you can see an increase in self-confidence in some children!**

Don't think that chess is only suitable for intellectually strong children or children who naturally excel in learning. Children with ASD (Autism Spectrum Disorder), dyslexia, dyscalculia, ADHD, behavioral disorders, or emotional problems can be quite good at chess! The longer they play chess, the more their self-confidence grows, and the better they learn to control their emotions.

Children who don't believe in themselves (anymore) find solace in the idea that even the Pawn – the smallest piece on the chessboard – can become a Queen!

1.2. Mathematical Thinking

When we look at the development goals for preschool age, we primarily focus on the subject area of "space". However, mathematical concepts are also addressed: the value of the chess pieces, for example, is expressed in numbers.

Preschoolers regularly count how many pieces they have captured, compare them with their opponent, and count again.

We practice concepts such as next to, in front of, behind, straight, diagonal, forward, backward, as far as possible, etc. These concepts are not fully ingrained at the age of 4 or 5, but they are introduced through play. The mathematical vocabulary is expanded by using terminology such as "broken line, diagonal"... Spatial awareness is developed through chess....

1.3. Brain Development

Studies show that during chess, metabolism increases, nerve cells become more active and start communicating with each other. Networks are activated during chess, according to clinical neuropsychologist Erik Scherder (website sport.nl).

"I'm mentioning only a few areas frequently used during chess. The frontal lobe for planning, flexible thinking, letting go of previous thoughts, and learning from mistakes. And the parietal lobe, which is essential for information processing."

The connections between these brain regions enable communication and the sharing of information necessary for a task. Chess helps children think better, analyze better,

concentrate, and develop a strategy to reach a solution. The fact that these connections are more dynamic in the brains of chess experts than in those of novice chess players indicates that regular chess playing can improve brain communication.

"Chess is fantastic for everyone, especially for children and young people. By playing chess, you build up a cognitive reserve that you can tap into later when your brain declines, to protect yourself against age-related diseases", says Scherder.

2. Considerations

2.1. Why Learn in This Way?

You might think: why working with all those mini games and not just explain the rules of chess in an ordinary instruction? This approach can work, and I did it for a few years in a first-grade class. Spending ten minutes a day presenting something on an instruction board and doing some exercises is possible. You can capture their attention during that short instruction time. By the end of the school year, the 6-7-year-olds knew the basic rules.

However, if you want to try it with younger children, you need a narrative framework. When I tried to introduce the chess rules to preschoolers, I noticed that whole-class instruction or practice didn't work well. Preschoolers require a different approach.

They must feel it, experience it, live it, be stimulated by the drawing, the story, or a character so that it remains captivating. This book originated from that experience! This picture book is a mix of a story and chess rules so that preschoolers are introduced to the world of chess. The characters are lively and imaginative. Even the smallest chess piece - the Pawn - plays an important role in the story.

2.2. Why Start So Young?

Wouldn't it be better to wait until they are seven or eight years old? I have noticed that it is beneficial to introduce this in kindergarten. On the one hand, there is more time available in the weekly schedule of a kindergarten class, as the curriculum of a first-grade class is often packed. On the other hand, it is an opportunity to teach preschoolers something new that can be used as differentiation in elementary school for children who have completed their tasks or need an extra challenge. Imagine a child moving on to first grade already able to count to 10 or read. Why not engage this child with a chessboard or chess exercises?

Furthermore, there is a third good reason: mature pre-schoolers, gifted preschoolers, preschoolers with concentration problems, insecure children, etc. can be identified while introducing chess. My observations during chess lessons often confirm the perceptions that kindergarten teachers already have of their children. "This child has insight, thinks ahead, has good spatial perception... or "This child has difficulty concentrating, gets angry quickly, can't handle losing..."

3. Getting Started: Introducing the Chess Pieces One By One Through Games

3.1. Preliminary

The more attention you can give to each child, the more you can adapt to their level. As a parent, grandparent, therapist, or chess coach, you can easily work with this book.

In the other part of this toolbox, I address teachers or facilitators who work with a group, so they can easily start playing chess and discover the added value of this game! In the books of the Steps Method, you can find a lot of background information about the developmental psychology of children who play chess.

If you feel that the child can handle more instruction, you will find numerous games and exercises in this manual that are aimed at chess trainers.

I tried to come up with variations in my lessons because I work with very young children (+4) and want to keep preschoolers engaged. Some games that work well with preschoolers have been included in this book with permission from Cor van Wijgerden. The goal of each game is described alongside the chess piece being introduced.

Take the time to practice the games! **The intention is to repeat a game,** especially when the child enjoys it. So don't rush to the next game or a new chess piece too quickly.

If a game is perceived as difficult, take a break and play a lighter game in between, then return to the exercise later.

In kindergarten, I take two years to introduce all the basic rules by repeating a game every week and building from there. As an individual coach, you can easily follow the child's pace. Some children learn quickly, while others need more time. Try to sense what your child needs. Choose which game will have the most success for each chess piece or play them all for variation.

However, don't expect a four-year-old preschooler to have an overview of the chessboard. A child of that age doesn't have that perspective yet. They are mainly focused on the intriguing pieces and not so much on the flow of the game, attacking moves, or checkmate. This comes in a later stage.

Nevertheless, it is good to bring their attention to it. The different possibilities of a move can be visually represented to gain insight into the game. You can do this by placing objects on the squares where the chess piece is allowed to move. It could be a disc, block, bottle cap, or coin.

You can even use the tiles of your kitchen floor or terrace to physically experience what we mean by straight or diagonal lines. Usually, I demonstrate on a small chessboard what we will practice, and then we play as chess pieces on a large chessboard. This allows the children to better understand the concepts and reinforce the rules. The children are invited to step into the role of the characters, which helps them recall and apply the chess rules from memory. **This is called active learning.**

If you want to work with individual coaching in this way, please refer to the games listed on the reverse side of this toolbox.

One of the most difficult chess pieces to introduce is the Horse*, it's the only chess piece that can jump into eight possible directions.

With young children, the Knight's move is often a challenging concept. I have searched for countless variations (and rhymes) to teach them that move. The choice for the rhyme that is now in the book was made with the children. It sounded the most beautiful to them and was best understood.

The support of the picture book combined with the rhyme will definitely add value!

The Knight being the correct chess term used

3.2. Special Moves Or Positions

These are not covered in this book. Once the preschooler knows and has practiced the basic rules, they will be ready to tackle more extensive exercises through other chess books for young children.

The chess book you have in your hands has been deliberately created for the very young ones. Its purpose is to stimulate their curiosity and teach them the moves of the chess pieces in a playful manner.

3.3. Point Value

Chess pieces are assigned a point value to demonstrate that some pieces are more powerful than others. This point value is not arbitrarily chosen but based on the experience of chess players over hundreds of years.

Young children are not initially concerned with this point value; for them, "capturing" is important. They may capture a Pawn but lose their Queen in the process... and they don't mind. Until they learn that it is better to protect the important pieces.

In my experience, some preschoolers become fixated on this point value because they think they need to collect the most "points". It can be a goal in itself as a game; who can collect 20 points the fastest? But it sometimes distracts them from the real goal: winning by checkmating the King! Therefore, you can choose not to discuss point values yet and only introduce it after presenting all the chess pieces.

Why do you talk about the point value?

- To emphasize the importance of strong and weaker pieces.

- To gain understanding of "trading" in chess; for example, you capture the Queen but in doing so, you lose a Bishop. In that case, you still made a gain.

> The Pawn is worth one point.
>
> The Knight is worth three points.
>
> The Bishop is worth three points.
>
> The Rook is worth five points.
>
> The Queen is worth nine or ten points.
>
> The King is infinitely valuable because if you trap it, you lose the game.

3.4. Rows and Files

At the bottom of the chessboard, you will find letters, and on the sides, you have numbers. This allows for easier naming of squares, such as "Place your chess piece on e1".

Horizontally, we refer to rows, and vertically, we call them files (or columns). A chessboard is set up correctly when the white square h1 is located in the bottom right corner, the white chess pieces are on rows 1 and 2, and the black pieces are on rows 7 and 8.

Introducing this information to preschoolers is difficult and not essential to playing the game. You can certainly share it if the child shows interest, but I included it here so that as a guide, you can position the chess pieces correctly. This is important for some of the games.

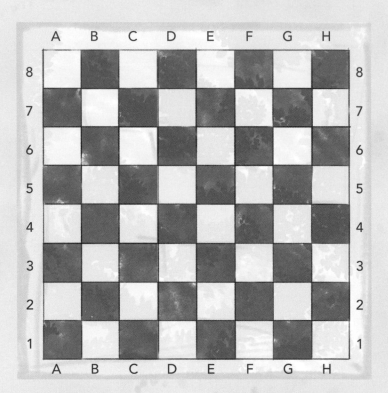

3.5. Playing With the King

(see pages 32 to 37 of the picture book)

Let's agree now that
we won't capture the Kings!
You can capture them,
but the game is not over yet!

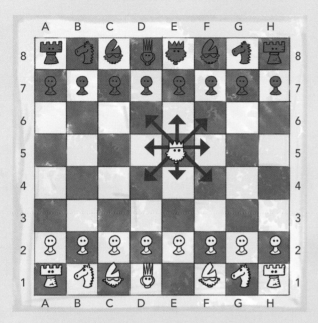

The starting position on the chessboard: revisit the pages about the steps of the King and discover together with your child where it starts on the chessboard: the White King is on the black square e1, and the Black King is on the white square e8.

The King can move one step in any direction, and then he needs to take a rest.

Examine each King to see which squares this chess piece can move to on the chessboard. You can mark those squares by placing a disk (or another object) on them.

When starting and finishing any chess game do not forget to shake hands with your opponent.

The following games are aimed at practicing:

Introducing spatial concepts: forward, sideways, backward, next to, diagonal...

Learning and applying the concept of "capturing" (first "waking up," then "grabbing," and finally using the correct term, "capturing").

Understanding that Kings cannot be placed next to each other and, therefore, cannot capture each other.

Learning to take turns by moving the King one step at a time.

Game 1 K

The Black King Among the Sleeping Chess Pieces.

Here are some tips for Game 1:

1.   Focus on teaching the child how to make and verbalize one step in all directions. Emphasize that the goal is to understand and communicate the movement of the King.

2.   When a piece is not being captured, point it out to the child and assess whether they have understood the game correctly. This helps reinforce the concept that capturing is optional and not always necessary.

3.   Teach the child that capturing means gently pushing the opponent's piece off its square and replacing it with their own piece. The accompanying rhyme can aid in remembering this concept.

4.   Encourage the child to handle the chess pieces carefully and avoid knocking them over. If pieces are accidentally displaced, it becomes difficult to track their original positions. Place captured pieces neatly at the side of the chessboard.

5.   Don't rush to the next game too quickly. Play this game frequently and allow the child to become comfortable with the movements of the King before moving on to new challenges.

"This chess piece I must take, because that spot is mine to make."

Description: In this game, you will introduce the story of King Black who goes for a morning walk in his land and wakes up all the chess pieces. They rise and leave the chessboard.

Objective: The goal of the game is for the King to "wake up" (capture) all the white chess pieces as quickly as possible.

Materials: You will need the Black King piece and white chess pieces or other objects like discs, bottle caps, or blocks to represent the chess pieces.

The course of the game is as follows: Place the Black King on the chessboard and place the objects (chess pieces) on random squares.

Take turns controlling the Black King.

Work together to 'wake up' (capture) all the chess pieces.

Verbally express each step the King takes, for example: "He now takes one step diagonally" or "I move him one step backwards." Encourage the child to use the same language. Understanding the concept of a 'diagonal' step may be new for a young child.

Continuously verbalize your thoughts, observations, and actions during the game.

If things are going well, add the White King to the game. The White King will disrupt the Black King's game. The 'sleeping' pieces now become 'white' chess pieces.

Explain that from now on, we will only talk about 'capturing' and not 'waking up' pieces. During this game, the White King will protect his pieces. Discuss how he can do this by standing next to a white chess piece. This way, the Black King cannot capture that piece because two Kings cannot stand next to each other.

Take turns playing, starting with White and then Black.

Game 2 K

The King Chooses His Soldiers

Objective: The Kings try to gather as many soldiers for their army as possible. The game ends when all the soldiers are removed from the board.

Preparation: Take a look at the page in the book that explains the rules for the King. The two Kings should not be too close to each other (there must be at least one square in between). The objective is to collect as many pieces as possible while adhering to this rule

Materials: Take the White and Black Kings and sixteen small discs or blocks. Do not use Pawns or other chess pieces; use something neutral to focus primarily on capturing.

Gameplay: Place all the markers on random squares on the chessboard, with approximately eight markers on each half. Position the two Kings in their starting positions. Shake hands and say "Have fun." One player controls the Black King, and the other player controls the White King. The White King starts the game. Take turns making moves with the Kings, ensuring that they capture a marker as quickly as possible. The player with the most soldiers collected wins.

Variation: Place all the discs in the center of the chessboard (four rows of four).

Remember to make the game enjoyable and encourage the child to strategize and make decisions during their turns.

Game 3 K

Treasure Hunt!

Objective: The Kings must maintain distance while trying to reach the treasure as quickly as possible. Their helpers occasionally build a wall when they get too close to each other.

Preparation: Explain that there is a treasure on the chessboard. It can be anything: a doll, a car, a dinosaur, a real treasure chest, a cup, etc. Which King will reach it first? Place the treasure on the 4th rank and switch colors in the next game: the white player becomes black and vice versa.

Materials: A White King, a Black King, and a treasure. For each King, you'll also need eight colored discs (or paper strips) to build a protective wall around the King.

Gameplay: Place the White King on c1 and the Black King on g1. Put the treasure on e7. This way, both Kings are equidistant from the treasure. They take turns, with white going first as usual. When you think one King is getting too close to another King, you can protect your King by placing the eight discs (or the strip) around your King to create a protective wall. This will help the other King see which squares it's not allowed to enter. There should always be an empty square between the Kings. After playing a few times, you might be able to manage without the visual wall. If a King does end up in the danger zone, it's defeated.

It's possible that neither King can capture the treasure because they approach it simultaneously while maintaining the required distance. In this case, the Kings will share the treasure! In a real game of chess, it's also possible for the game to end in a draw. This occurs in a stalemate or when the opponent has insufficient chess pieces left. We call this a draw.

Children may sometimes take detours, allowing one of them to reach the treasure faster than the other. Discuss afterwards what the shortest or fastest route was. This game can be played multiple times, but they will quickly figure out the fastest route unless you introduce obstacles that the Kings must navigate around.

Game 4 K

"King, Watch Out for Cars!"

Objective: The King must not put himself in danger. He must watch where he walks while trying to reach the other side as quickly as possible.

You'll notice that I'm not formulating the goal as "learning to give check" or "checkmating". Because putting a King in danger is actually called "putting in check." It can be difficult for these beginner chess players to do it intentionally. Unless we use cars! Then they understand it very well.

Children often accidentally discover that their King is in danger. They are focused on capturing pieces. However, it doesn't hurt to remind them that they need to protect their King and take action first. At that moment, the rule of "once you make a move, it's done" no longer applies. A King must not put himself in danger, so he must be moved to safety first.

Preparation: Tell the child that we are going to play with cars on the chessboard. It may seem a bit strange, but there used to be a chariot in the game of chess! Ask the child what "danger" means... maybe they can relate it to traffic situations; we also watch out for cars. We don't walk in the middle of the street or cross without looking carefully. Kings should do the same.

When the King moves, he must be careful not to step into a dangerous street. The reverse can also happen: if a car ends up in the King's street, the King must move quickly.

The cars move like Rooks, in straight lines. Demonstrate this clearly. They don't just move diagonally or zigzag across the board.

Materials: The chessboard, the 2 Kings, and 2 small toy cars.

   x2

Gameplay: The Kings start in their respective positions. Two cars are placed on the chessboard, for example, on a3 and h6. White begins, and then it's black's turn.

As a player, you can choose what to move: your King or one of the cars, even if it has just been moved. The car is neutral; it doesn't belong to White or Black, but it can move in straight lines (like a Rook). This allows you to play offensively or try to reach the other side first. Be careful: a car adjacent to a King can be captured by the King! But if the car is too far away, you'll need to move the King to safety in the next turn, as it would be in a dangerous street.

Regularly express what you see: "Oops, I'm in danger, or I'm putting you in danger!" If the car is placed on a rank (street) where a King is located, then the King must be moved to safety first! There is no other option; the King must be rescued before anything else.

When playing the game again, switch colors. Initially, white may have an advantage, but as the child starts thinking strategically, they can still win with black.

In this game too, it may happen that the Kings remain stuck in place because a car keeps moving to "cut off" the opposing King horizontally from the part of the board that lies in front of him. Pause the game and discuss what can still happen. You can even attach two strips in a cross shape on the roof of the car to clearly show the child that a straight line is formed horizontally and vertically from the car. Children don't always think about attacking vertically.

Also, point out other dangers to them: when they flee from one car, they must also keep an eye on the other car.

Finally: A checkmate position can accidentally occur. The King is at the edge, one car attacks him on that path, and the other car covers the adjacent path so the King cannot find safety there either (we call it a "staircase checkmate"). In that case, pause the game and show them the illustration from the book where the King lies on the "losing mat" (page 37). The King has nowhere to go; he is lost!

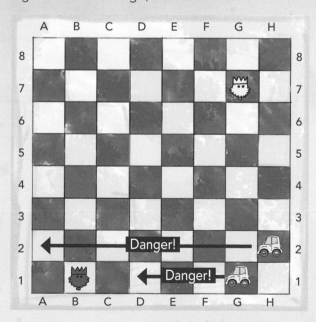

3.6. Playing with the Rook

(page 38 of the picture book)

It slides across both colors,
First white, then black, again white and black.
It moves sideways or straight ahead, look...
it steps right over a pedestrian crossing!

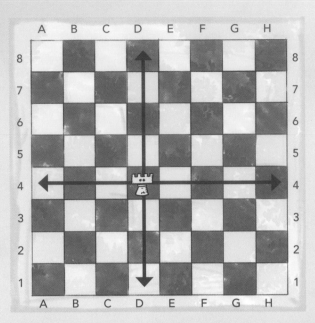

The starting position on the chessboard: a Rook stands on each corner. The White Rooks are on a1 and h1, the black ones on a8 and h8. Take the picture book page 38 and reread the rhymes so that the child hears what a Rook can do. The Rook is straight and tall. That means it moves in straight lines and can slide as far as it wants: forward, backward, or sideways. If it encounters another chess piece on its path, it can capture it. It cannot jump over it. Naturally, it doesn't capture pieces of its own color!

Changing direction is not easy; the Rook must first stop and wait for its next turn. How do you teach this to young children?

You can refer to the game with the cars, which drive in straight lines. It can't just take a turn! If we want to turn the car into another street, we often have to stop, look carefully, and then turn. After that, we can continue driving. That's how it is with a Rook too. If it wants to change direction, it must wait for its next turn!

You can also compare it to the Bee-bot or other programming materials if the child has already encountered them.

The principle of going straight, stopping, and turning is then known or quickly understood. In addition, it helps to visually mark the path the Rook will take. Let the child use strips, bars, or blocks to mark the path. The Rook's path is straight. If you make a turn in one move, you would have to crack the bar or bend the strip... the Rook would then be making a broken line. It's incredible how quickly some children adopt this wording during the game: "No, you're making a broken line, that's not allowed!"

When you make the path visually, the child will notice that a cross is usually formed originating from the Rook. For preschoolers who can already count, you can let them discover that the Rook can always go to fourteen squares, no matter where you place it.

Changing places in one turn is called "castling" (involving the Rook and the King). However, it is best to introduce this concept later as too much information might cause younger chess players to lose interest. We want to keep the child engaged, so it's advisable to cover "castling" in a different children's chess book or website. (Refer to the tips at the back of the book for recommendations).

The following games focus on practicing:
Introducing spatial concepts: forward, backward, step sideways in the other direction.
Understanding that Rooks can move "as far as needed" without changing direction (not making a broken line).
Understanding that they cannot jump over obstacles or walls.
Understanding that you stay on the square where you capture an opponent's chess piece.
Learning to take turns by making one move at a time.
Collaboratively planning and visualizing a path. Which is the fastest route?
Executing the planned path using the Rook.
Reaching a predetermined square as the final goal.

When starting and finishing any chess game do not forget to shake hands with your opponent.

Game 1 R

Programming the Rook

Objective: The White and Black Rooks compete against each other to see which Rook reaches the other side first.

Materials: A White and a Black Rook, and a few blocks that obstruct the path.

Gameplay: Explain that the Rooks need to reach the other side as quickly as possible. Place the white Rook on c1 and the Black Rook on f8, or experiment with another starting position. However, don't place them directly across from each other, as White would immediately be able to capture the Black Rook since White always starts.

You can place some obstacles on the path (blocks on certain squares) to make the Rooks change direction. Use a ruler or a strip of paper to indicate the straight lines on the board.

Now take turns moving the Rooks. Verbally express your actions each time. Emphasize that if you want to change direction, you must wait for the next turn before moving your Rook sideways.

When the child is ready, you can make the game a bit more challenging by mentioning that they need to watch out for each other. If both Rooks are in the same line, they can capture each other.

Something more challenging?

- Using two Rooks per color is considerably more difficult, as they'll encounter each other sooner. Remove the obstacles if it becomes too complex.

- Or, if you add a King to the game, can they still accomplish the goal? Experiment with the chess pieces the child is familiar with. Discuss which chess pieces need to watch out for each other (pieces of the same color are part of the same "family" so they cannot be captured by each other). Repeat this information frequently during practice.

Game 2 R

Rook, Find the Best Path!

Objective: In this game, the goal is not simply to reach the other side with eight possible destination squares. Now, the Rook needs to land on a specific predetermined square! Explain that you will work together and discuss the best path. You will listen to each other and realize that there are multiple possibilities, expanding your thinking.

Materials: A White Rook, several blocks obstructing the path, a destination (treasure, e.g., a coin), strips of paper or rulers to create a visual straight path.

 x8

Gameplay: Start by placing the treasure on the chessboard and position the Rook on rank 1. The goal is for the Rook to reach the treasure via the shortest path. Create an obstacle using the blocks. Have the child lay out the path using the strips of paper or rulers. Is this the fastest path? In how many moves can the Rook reach the treasure? How many times does it need to change direction? What other paths could you choose?

You can repeat this game many times, experimenting with the position of the Rook, the treasure, or the blocks. Some children might start thinking insightfully during this process, as placing the blocks requires careful consideration.

Something more challenging?

- If you wish, you can use numbers or multiple colored squares that need to be traversed in a specific order. Prepare this sequence next to the board (or draw it on cards beforehand) so that the child can see the pattern they need to follow.

- Instead of colors, you can also use numbers. This way, numbers are practiced in a playful manner.

Game 3 R
Collecting Discs

Objective: Collect as many discs or blocks as possible while ensuring that our Rook is not captured. The game ends when all the discs are gone, even if a Rook can still be captured.

Materials: Chessboard, one white Rook, one black Rook, a number of objects or discs to "capture".

Gameplay: Place the White Rook on a1 and the Black Rook on h8. Scatter the objects on random squares on the board.

Players take turns moving the Rooks according to the basic rules. If a Rook lands on a square with an object, the player can take that object and "capture" it. You can repeat a chant and practice correctly moving the object to place the Rook in that spot.

The game continues until all the objects have been captured from the board. The child can count to see who has collected the most.

"This chess piece I must take,
because that spot is mine to make."

Something more challenging?

When this game runs smoothly, you can introduce both Rooks to the game in their starting positions, which are the corners of the chessboard. Show the child that the Rooks are directly facing each other. This means that the White Rook could capture the Black Rook immediately. To prevent this, place a disc on lines a and h. Clearly explain to the child that the Rooks cannot capture each other because the disc is in between them. But once the discs are gone, they are facing each other! The next player's turn will allow them to capture the opponent's Rook.

Don't be surprised if the child, despite your warning, chooses to immediately capture a disc; preschoolers often do that... They really want to conquer it! The realization that they lose a Rook by doing so comes later.

Game 4 R
King, Watch Out for the Rooks!

Objective: Now that the Rook's moves have been practiced, some additional thinking is introduced by bringing the King into the game! Here's what they need to do:

- The King must reach the endpoint (a treasure).
- The King must not be captured.
- The King must not be put in danger (by placing it in the path of the opponent's Rook).
- If the King is in danger, it must be brought to safety.

Information beforehand: With this game, you can introduce the concept of "check": if you place your Rook on the line (or street) where your opponent's King is, you are attacking that King. We call it "check". What can the King do then? Move away from that line, hide behind a wall if it's nearby, or place another Rook in between. Or if the King happens to be next to the attacking Rook, it can capture it! Demonstrate this on a small chessboard. The goal is not for the child to master the concept of "check" after this game. Give them more time for that! But they can become familiar with these moves in a playful way.

Materials: The White Rook and King, the Black Rook and King, a treasure.

Gameplay: Place a white rook on a1 and the white king in its starting position, e1. The black rook starts on h8, and the black king on e8. Place an object or "treasure" on f6 where the white king should end his walk and on d3 for the black king. Take turns making moves with your Rook or King. The first King to reach the treasure wins, even if the player has lost a Rook. Point out to the child that the game becomes more challenging for the King when they lose a Rook. If the

King is in check, their priority in the next move should be to save the King.

You can replay the game and place obstacles on certain squares to make it even more exciting. After each game, switch colors: the white player becomes black, and vice versa.

3.7. Playing with the Bishop

point value

3

(page 40 of the picture book)

Refer to the story again so that the child hears that the Bishop always stays on the same color. He finds his shoes very important. If he is wearing white shoes, he only stays on white. That's why a Bishop with black shoes has also been introduced because you always need a Bishop on both colors. Show both White Bishops and place them on different colors. Then show the two Black Bishops. This way, the child sees that there are four Bishops in the game. Study the funny hat, which looks like Saint-Nicolas' miter, patron saint of children. We see a diagonal stripe on the hat, which reminds us that the Bishop always moves diagonally.

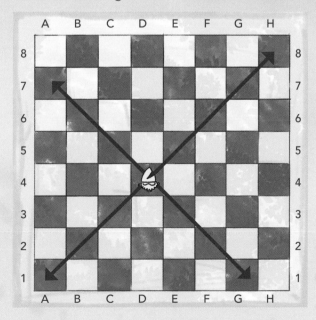

It is important to spend enough time on the understanding of "diagonal".

The squares on the chessboard touch each other at the corners and form a diagonal line: we follow the same color,

so that means we walk to the corner of a square and step onto the next square. You can examine the Bishop's shoes in detail. They are pointy and refer to a corner of a chess square.

If you have a chessboard pattern in your kitchen or on your terrace, take your child for a walk and walk on the diagonal squares. After a while, you can let the child walk independently. Note: do not let them hop from one leg to the other, landing on a black square, for example, from b2 to c3 to b4 to c5 ... Then they don't realize they're moving diagonally. Hopping in a zigzag manner is not allowed; the body needs to rotate and change direction like a robot.

The following games focus on practicing:
Introducing spatial concepts: diagonally forward, diagonally backward.
Understanding that Bishops can move "as far as necessary".
Knowing that Bishops stay on their own color throughout the game.
Understanding that you stay on the square where you capture a chess piece.
Learning to take turns by making one move.

You will notice that there are fewer games written out in this section. **Some games from the Rook section can be repeated with the Bishop**. I'm thinking of "Programming the Bishop", "Finding the Best Path", or "Collecting Discs". You will see that the child quickly grasps the task. Only the diagonal movement is new.

Tip: When setting up the chessboard, you need to think carefully about which color the bishop should start and end on since the bishop always stays on its own color! So, you cannot give a black squared bishop the task of ending on a white square or picking up the disc on a white square.

In the game "Collecting Discs," you need to place an equal number of discs on black and white squares to ensure fair chances. Unless you have the white and black bishops moving on the same color. Then it's a race to see who reaches the treasure first.

Game 1 B

Bishop, Beware of the King!

Objective: The child practices sliding the Bishop over the correct color and following the diagonal lines. When the Bishop gets too close to the King, the King can capture it. In the first game, you play as the King.

Materials: A white Bishop on f1 (white), the Black King on d4 (black).

Gameplay: If you want to play this game on a small chessboard, we can't really call it a tagging game. Explain to the child that this time, you won't take turns, but instead, you'll practice the path of the Bishop. Show them how it's done first.

Let the child guide the White Bishop on a stroll. The Bishop needs to change direction ten times. But it can't go back and forth on the same diagonal line three times in a row! However, if it passes next to the Black King, the King can capture the Bishop. Is the King alert enough to intervene in time?

Game 2 B

The Bishop Takes on Two Rooks

You will notice that the child gets better and better at playing with the chess pieces, especially if you don't put too many "characters" on the board at once. In a chess match, a timer is usually used. It's not a bad idea to incorporate it as a game element. Not to stress the child, but to explain that it's good to agree on how long the game will last. Some chess players can spend hours on the same game if they don't use a clock. The longest game ever lasted 24 hours and 30 minutes, a day and a night! The goal is simple: the Bishop must be captured before time runs out; otherwise, the Bishop wins.

Materials: Two Black Rooks and one White Bishop, a timer or an hourglass (start with 10 minutes).

Gameplay: Set up the chess pieces in their starting positions. The White Bishop starts and begins its move. Then it's black's turn to make a move. Black's goal is, of course, to capture the Bishop with their Rook before the time runs out. Can they achieve this?

Game 3 B

Running in Circles, Get Back to Your Starting Position As Fast As Possible

Objective: Make the chess pieces run around a wall and return to their starting position as quickly as possible. They should follow the correct path: the Bishop on diagonal lines and the Rook on straight lines. Show in advance the direction in which they should start (clockwise).

Materials: Chessboard, a White Bishop and Rook, and a Black Bishop and Rook. In the center of the chessboard, place a wall made of blocks or Pawns.

Gameplay: The White Bishop starts on a1, the Rook on b1, the Black Bishop starts on h8, and the Rook on g8. White can start and make a move. The objective of the game is to "run" around the wall (in a clockwise direction) and return to the starting position as quickly as possible. Who is the fastest? Capturing is not allowed. Afterward, switch sides and play again to see who can achieve the fastest time. Capturing is not allowed. Afterwards change color!

When starting and finishing any chess game do not forget to shake hands with your opponent.

3.8. Playing with the Queen

point value
9

(page 42 of the picture book)

Straight lines and diagonal stripes,
or when she stands in the middle of the board.
She can reach up to twenty-seven squares.
No other chess piece can match that!

Take the picture book, page 43, and read the story again. Look at this illustration and tell how much the Queen loves to start on her own color. She has put on her most beautiful dress for that. This way, we can remember where she starts on the chessboard: next to the King on her own color. Since the Rook and Bishop are already known, it is very easy to transition to the dame (queen). She can move to the squares used by both the Rook and Bishop. Demonstrate this first on a small board. Place a Rook on d5 and let the child use colored discs to indicate the squares it can move to. Then replace the Rook with a Bishop and mark this path with different discs. Finally, replace the Bishop with a Queen and tell them that she can do both of these things together! The Queen is a powerful

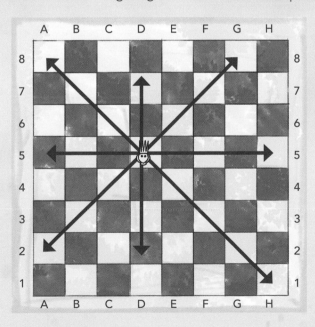

chess piece, let the child count the squares it can move to!

These games help practice:
Further practicing spatial concepts.
Looking at the path being taken: diagonal, sideways, straight, or backward.
Changing direction effectively: stopping first, then continuing on the next turn.
Being aware of dangers.
Learning to cope with frustration (the more chess pieces on the board, the more challenging the game becomes, and the more likely you are to miss something).

Game 1 Q

Celebration with the Queen

Objective: Explain that the Queen is hosting a celebration in her castle and personally picking up her friends to join in. She visits them one by one and takes them in her carriage. The child can fantasize about the type of celebration: a pancake party, a coffee gathering, a fries feast... They find it super exciting! But... will they arrive on time for the celebration?

Materials: A White Queen and other white chess pieces. A timer or an hourglass can make the game more exciting. All "guests" must be picked up before the time runs out.

Gameplay: The Queen goes for a walk and picks up one chess piece at a time. This picked-up chess piece is placed aside (in the carriage). The Queen continues her journey. Since there's no other player, the Queen plays the entire time. You can choose to work together and take turns with the Queen to make a move. This way, the child learns to stop when changing direction.

Observe how the child approaches the game: Do they use both diagonal and straight lines? Is there a particular strategy in picking up the pieces?

When using a timer, you can gradually reduce the time available. Another approach is to pick up the chess pieces in a specific order, for example, start with those with the highest point value like the Rook and then the Bishop. Will you manage to pick them all up in time for the party to start?

Game 2 Q

The Festive Table Is Set!

The party is starting for real. All the guests are gathered around the table, choosing the tastiest treats.

Objective: Who can capture the discs without getting captured themselves? Jumping over the discs is not allowed.

Materials: A Queen and Rook of both colors, eight discs or blocks (representing delicious treats on the party table).

Gameplay: Place the Queens on their starting positions. The White Rook is placed on b1, and the Black Rook on g8. The discs are placed in the middle of the chessboard (as shown in the illustration). White starts, followed by black. The game stops when all the discs are taken. Have any chess pieces been captured? Who has managed to capture the most delicious treats? Add up the point value of the remaining chess pieces and the number of captured discs. For instance, if white has four discs and their Queen left, they have a total of 13 points. Switch colors and play the game again. Then tally up the final scores.

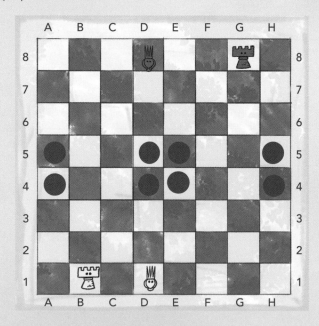

Something more challenging?

Add a second Rook for both colors.

Game 3 Q

The Starting Position

Objective: Practice the positioning of the chess pieces using all the pieces we have learned.

Materials: All the chess pieces we have learned so far for both colors: Rook, Bishop, Queen, and King.

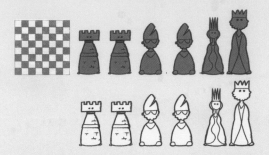

Gameplay: Place the white chess pieces on the first rank, deliberately mixing them up. Ensure that one Bishop is on a white square and the other Bishop on a black square! Do the same with the black pieces on the eighth rank.

Now, take turns making moves with the goal of bringing the chess pieces back to their correct starting positions as quickly as possible. You cannot go past the halfway point of the chessboard, so you cannot capture each other's pieces. Who can correctly position all the chess pieces first? Which squares remain? Those are reserved for the Knights!

3.9. From Pawn to Queen!

point value
1

"But when you reach the other side,
a true miracle will occur.
You transform into another chess piece,
it's truly something special!"

The Pawn is more challenging than you might think! Refer to the picture book starting from page 44 and pay attention to the illustrations as a memory aid. You can even perform a puppet show where the King interacts with Pompon Pawn.

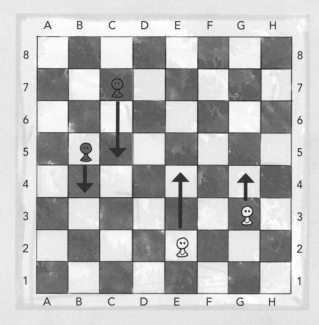

At first, Pompon Pawn is unhappy because she doesn't get to do much: only move forward! Build up the rules gradually. Focus on the story as it helps young children remember. Make sure the child understands everything.

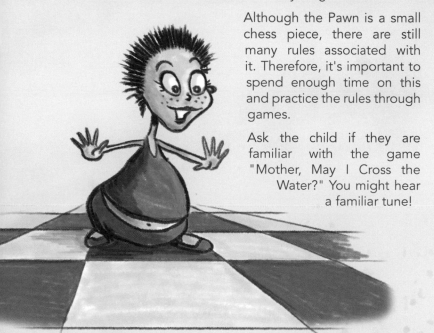

Although the Pawn is a small chess piece, there are still many rules associated with it. Therefore, it's important to spend enough time on this and practice the rules through games.

Ask the child if they are familiar with the game "Mother, May I Cross the Water?" You might hear a familiar tune!

Refer to the concept of the "other side," which is the destination. You're not allowed to go back or move backward. The same applies to Pawns: they can only move forward toward the other side. It's crucial for them to reach that side because they transform into a stronger piece!

To demonstrate capturing diagonally, you can twist pipe cleaners (wire) around the Pawns, forming "arms." Open the arms wide to emphasize that the Pawn captures diagonally in front of itself.

Practice this by standing opposite each other and stretching out your arms. This way, you can "catch" each other. But Pawns are not allowed to do it that way! They must open their arms and capture diagonally.

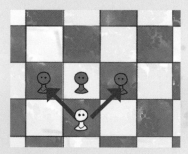

This allows them to change ranks. Pompon Pawn is super happy about this! Emphasize this aspect, that changing ranks can only happen by capturing.

In conclusion, this book explains the fundamental basic rules. When the child has progressed further, it's recommended to consult another book or website to learn about the "en passant" rule. This rule allows a Pawn to capture "in passing" by moving diagonally forward to capture an opponent's Pawn. It's an important rule to learn, but we don't burden the young beginners with it just yet.

The following games focus on:
Concepts: reaching the other side, moving forward in a line, capturing diagonally.
Counting up to two or making a "double move."
Introducing the concept of promotion: the Pawn transforms into another chess piece when it reaches the other side.
Understanding the concept of a "stronger chess piece": the Queen is the strongest, followed by the Rook, Bishop, and Knight.
Emphasizing forward thinking and avoiding impulsive reactions.
Introducing the term "touch".

Game 1 P

Crackle-Boom-Woosh...
A Miracle Happens!

Objective: Practice moving Pawns and have the child verbalize which chess piece the Pawn promotes to when it reaches the other side.

Materials: A chessboard, two White Pawns and two Black Pawns.

Gameplay: Explain that you will practice the correct steps by taking turns making moves. Repeat the rules: Pawns move one or two squares forward from their starting position, and after that, they move one square forward in the same line, never backward!

Place the two White Pawns on b2 and c2 and the Black Pawns on f7 and g7, ensuring they are not directly opposite each other on the board. They should not be able to capture each other yet and must be able to move freely to the other side. The focus of this practice is on Pawn movement and promotion across the board. Ask the child which chess piece they choose when the Pawn reaches the other side. (The Pawn "promotes" to a Queen, Rook, Bishop, or Knight.)

You can intentionally make a few mistakes to see if the child understands the rules and follows the game: move backward, move sideways or diagonally without capturing, continue moving two squares at a time, move backward, etc.

If this goes well, place the Pawns in different positions on

Game 2 P

Guess Who Gets Fooled?

Objective: The Pawns "awaken" and assess how many discs are on the line in front of them. Can they capture them? Or will they be fooled? How can they collect the most discs? Forward thinking is necessary. We introduce the term "touch": touching means making a move with the touched piece!

Materials: A small chessboard, four White Pawns, five discs.

Gameplay: Place the Pawns on b2, d2, f2, and h2. The player playing as white closes their eyes for a moment. The other player sets up the discs on the 3rd rank. The discs can be placed diagonally in front of a Pawn or directly in front. "Ready, eyes open! Guess, guess, guess, how many discs can you capture?" If the child looks and counts first, they might notice which action allows capturing the most discs (see the photo: a maximum of two). If the Pawn from b2 captures the disc on c3, there's only one move possible. Perhaps they responded too quickly? In this game, impulsive children can learn self-regulation. Introduce the concept of "touché": touching is moving! So, we need to think first without touching the chess pieces and only make the capture move when we're sure of it.

Game 3 P

Who Reaches the Other Side First?

Objective: The first to promote wins! You also win if your opponent can no longer move. Pay attention to capturing, which can only be done diagonally!

Materials: A small chessboard and all eight Pawns of both colors.

 x8 x8

Game progression: Place the Pawns in their starting positions. White starts and moves a Pawn forward. Then, it's black's turn. The game now revolves around capturing and being captured, or getting blocked. When two Pawns are facing each other and no other chess piece comes to their aid, they remain stuck.

Something more challenging?

The Black Queen against the White Pawns. Try to get a Pawn to the other side as quickly as possible. Through play, the child discovers the difference between being defended and undefended. If the child's Queen captures a Pawn and ends up diagonally opposite its opponent, it will lose its Queen quickly. However, if they handle the Queen well, they can capture many Pawns.

3.10. The Difficult Horse

point value
3

> I twist my snout and then watch out:
> I jump two steps forward and one aside
> That's happens when a Knight is untied.

Refer to page 48 of the picture book.

There are many variations used in teaching the horse's leap: two squares forward and one sideways or vice versa. Or one square in a straight line followed by one square diagonally. How difficult this is for young children! The concept of "diagonal" is completely beyond them. Trying to explain using the letter "L" is one possibility, but for preschoolers who are not yet working with letters, this is also not an entry point. In the Batsford publication of Chess for Kids by Sabrina Chevannes, the word "ka-ta-klop" is proposed as

rhythmic support. It's a fun idea, maybe it will work for your children.

I have tried various games but eventually came to the conclusion that it's better to keep it simple; one strategy, for example, through a rhyme.

It's important to explain that the horse always jumps to a different color on the chessboard and can turn its head in four directions. Show this on a small chessboard. I deliberately choose to position the head of the Horse in the direction it wants to go. This way, they concentrate on that path; they may turn the head again and again... Young children never think about making the horse jump backwards at first. That comes later naturally.

To practice the movements of the horse, you can play a few simple games with the child, pretending to be a horse. "Because a Horse's eyes are on the sides, it can't always see well ahead. Shall we try to experience how that feels?"

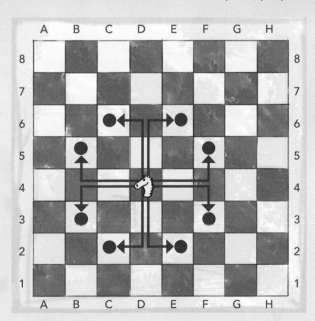

- Walk around with your nose up, maybe play a tagging game. Can we see each other well walking with our noses in the air? No! A Horse has the same problem. That's why it recites the verse in chess, so it always ends up in the right place. It can jump as if blind! Let's try that too? Recite the verse with your eyes closed and meanwhile take the steps: "I turn my snout and take two steps forward, now one to the side, that one's definitely required..." Open your eyes and look. You're performing a dance step!

- Do you have a hobbyhorse? Then you can practice the concept of "to the side" with it if it's not understood. The rider takes one step "to the side" when dismounting. The child sees that the eyes on the hobbyhorse are on the sides, those are the sides, emphasize that word.

19

The following games focus on:
Concepts: forward, sideways, addition.
The 4 "directions" in which the Knight can leap.
Role-playing and social interaction (taking directions and giving directions).
Memorizing the verse.
Following a path in the correct order or color.

Game 1 N
The Farmer Guards His Field

Objective: Visualize the position on the board by marking the landing squares for each leap of the Knight. Tell a story about a family that is worried about the Knight. It stands all alone in the meadow, and they are afraid it might escape! To prevent this, they decide to stand on all the spots where the Knight could land. Unfortunately, as evening approaches, they have to go to sleep and secretly hope that the horse will sleep too. But that's not the case...

Materials: A small chessboard, a White Knight, several discs or blocks (up to 8).

  maximum 8

Gameplay: Tell the story as described above. Place the Knight on the board, starting in the center. Then place a disc on all the squares the Knight can move to. Recite the verse as you do this. There are eight possibilities. Remove the discs and let the child perform the Knight's move on their own. There is no visual aid now.

Waking up to find the family's horse (knight) in a different position on the chessboard can be quite alarming. Upon closer examination, placing the horse on the side or in a corner reveals interesting insights. When the horse is positioned on the side, fewer discs are needed to mark a square, indicating its diminished maneuverability compared to when it's placed in the middle. In fact, placing the horse in a corner drastically limits its movement; significantly fewer discs can be placed compared to its placement in the middle. This observation leads to the conclusion that the knight is most effective when positioned in the middle of the chessboard. Utilize this concept to emphasize the importance of centralizing the knight in chess strategy, suggesting that 'If your horse is on the side, there is something wrong with it.' Thus, it becomes evident that the knight is strongest when positioned in the center of the chessboard."

And thus, the story repeats itself over and over again. After a few turns, let someone else play the Horse. Children find this game very enjoyable; they become fully immersed in it.

Game 2 N
Hey, Where Can I Leap To?!

Objective: Practice the Knight's leap and mark all the squares the Knight has visited. The Knight must not land on the same square twice.

Materials: A small chessboard, a Knight, many discs or blocks.

   Many players

Gameplay: Place the Knight in the center. Explain that you will take turns making the Knight jump. The goal is to visit as many squares as possible without landing on the same square twice. Place a disc where the Knight starts. The Knight cannot return to this square. Recite the verse when making the Knight's move. Can the Knight visit all the squares, or does it get stuck somewhere?

Game 3 N
The Horse is Hungry

This is a variation of the previous game. It is played in reverse: the game board is filled with discs. These represent the horse's food (e.g., carrots). Now the Knight will leap and try to eat all the carrots as quickly as possible.

Something more challenging?

- Let two Knights participate: one white and one black. Be careful, they can capture each other!
- Create cards with numbers or number representations (according to the level of your children). Scatter them across the board. The Knight must follow the correct path to collect the cards one by one. Make sure the child recites the verse and, therefore, takes the correct path. This is not an easy task. Sometimes, a detour must be taken to reach the correct square!
- There are fun apps available for practicing the Knight's leap. Consult your search engine for more information.

> When starting and finishing any chess game do not forget to shake hands with your opponent.

4. All Pieces Are in Place

How do you proceed once all the pieces have been covered? There are several possibilities:

- You can continue practicing with mini games (i.e. not all pieces on the board at once). In the next section, you will find some examples from the Steps Method by Rob Brunia and Cor van Wijgerden.

- Play a first full game, but assist the child in making choices. Try to verbalize a lot! Discuss the pros and cons of a move. Warn them if they overlook something important or provoke them by making a "wrong" move yourself … You can involve an older sibling to play together against you. Or is it the other way around, where you need to collaborate with your youngest child to defeat the eldest?

4.1. More Mini Games

Queen versus Knight

The White Queen needs to capture the Black Knight. They start in their initial positions. It's not an easy task! However, as they practice the game, they can succeed. For example, when the Knight is in a corner.

Bishop versus Pawns

Place three white Pawns on a2, b2, and c2. Across the board, there is a black Bishop on c8. White can start. The Pawn side wins if a Pawn promotes or if the Bishop is captured. The Bishop wins if all the Pawns are captured or if the last Pawn is blocked.

Promotion Game

Set up the eight white Pawns in their starting positions. Across the board, there is a Black Knight in its familiar spot, b8. When a Pawn reaches the opposite side, it promotes. This earns the white player a point. The Knight must capture as many Pawns as possible and prevent itself from being captured. After the first round, the players switch roles. Once this game is completed, the player with the most points is determined.

4.2. Websites and Instructional Videos

By consulting your search engine, you can find numerous sources of information about chess. Be cautious with chess programs that require practicing against a computer, as they can be challenging, especially for children. It's important to find a suitable platform where children don't get lost or lose interest. Therefore, I recommend https://lichess.org

While creating this book, I quickly realized that referring to some websites carries a risk. Links may work one day but not another. That's why I will share and update information on my own website to accommodate new developments or questions that arise. Visit www.kleuterschaken.be for this purpose.

On this site, you can watch instructional videos of the group games described in this book. The individual coach can also find photos of how to set up the various games. Some people prefer to see how it's done before trying it themselves. A picture is worth a thousand words. See how children enjoy the game, how the game progresses, and how to approach it.

Enjoy teaching and exploring the picture book together!

Tip: You can find a "losing mate" puzzle and a little dragon on many pages. Have you spotted them yet?